D1714528

Eileen Ballman was raised in Cheshire, Connecticut. She was the middle child in her large Irish Catholic family of eight. She's learned about life through her three distinct careers in sales, interior design, and teaching. After joining the military in the mid-seventies, she landed on the West Coast where she got married, raised her children, and lived joyfully for 22 years between Washington and Oregon. She and her family moved to North Carolina in 2000, and after retiring from teaching in 2012, she now resides in St Augustine, Florida, with her husband, Dave. She has two sons, Jake and Josh, and has a host of 'everywoman' friends who keep her happy and sane in her beloved beach town.

Eileen Ballman

FRAGMENTS OF AN EVERYWOMAN'S LIFE

AUSTIN MACAULEY PUBLISHERS™

LONDON • CAMBRIDGE • NEW YORK • SHARJAH

A CIP catalogue record for this title is available from the British Library.

ISBN 9781528936361 (Paperback)
ISBN 9781528936378 (Hardback)
ISBN 9781528968676 (ePub e-book)

www.austinmacauley.com

First Published (2019)
Austin Macauley Publishers Ltd
25 Canada Square
Canary Wharf
London
E14 5LQ

I would like to honor and give thanks to the generous women who acted as test readers. Their willingness to be truthfully forthright is a testament to their integrity. Their support has meant the world.

Thank you, Andrea DePreter, for your honesty and encouragement and for suggesting I revisit the book's ending which you felt I had rushed. I had, for it proved difficult to leave you, readers. Thank you, Jackie Siegel, for the relevant and enthusiastic calls and texts. Thank you, most of all for calling me right after you finished the book in order to share stories of your life now that the dam of caution was burst open.

Thanks to Angela Miller, Sandy Caster, Linda Carlson, Roberta Owen, and Barb Feldman for the insightful feedback of the first few chapters. Your frank comments offered eye-opening insights as to the diversity of responses I would receive from readers.

Thank you to my siblings who agreed to let me share a fragment from our childhood.

Thank you to my beloved lifetime friends, my kindred spirits, for your existence has made all the difference.

To my sons, Jake and Josh, who never worried about what I said in this memoir; they simply supported me for having the gumption to follow a dream.

To my husband, Dave, who doesn't always come across heroic in these musings but is honest enough to admit that it is the truth. His support has been unwavering.

Finally, thank you to all who reach out to every woman and every man through the arts. Whatever the shape this reaching-out takes, be it writing, painting, sculpting, music making, or dancing to name a few, your creative forces round out our complex lives, and you are so appreciated.

Table of Contents

When was the last time you listened to the stories of others?

Question put to the sick by a Native American Medicine Man.

Preface

A question to get us started: Do you ever talk to yourself? Well, if so, this just might be our first bonding moment; for I certainly do, and yes, at times it does the trick. At other times, however, it won't suffice because a fresh perspective is what's needed. My initial reaction for sound advice is to call upon a friend, yet sometimes I hesitate because I sense that he or she won't be able to advise me in a particularly unique circumstance. It is at such times that I think of you. Yes, **you.** No, you are not an imaginary friend; you are much more than that, but because we can't meet face to face, I have to content myself by reaching out to you through other avenues; in this case, through print. The fact of the matter is that I had begun reaching out to you years ago, but questioning receptivity, I've found myself delaying what I have now come to understand was inevitable. Naturally, I have asked myself what it is exactly that I am offering you in this relationship; why should you invest time getting to know me. How will I entice you to read fragments of a virtually unknown woman's life, for what on earth makes me believe you will gain something of significance and willingly write me back? Well, here is what I hope; I hope that this manner of epistolary discourse will prove useful for us all. First and foremost, I hope you will find some of the fragments of my life relatable, and as you read, your ability to relate will become a connection, a bond between us, and you will then feel the urge to write me back. The fact that we may not know each other extrinsically won't matter because we will find we are connected intrinsically. As fortunate as I am having the best of friends in times of crisis as well as celebration, it is those other times I am referring to where *you* dear reader come in. I sense you out there somewhere in the universe, existing who knows where but endeavoring to successfully navigate your own lives. This certainty of your existence has allowed me to move forward at times, in fact, for me your incontrovertible existence has proven downright essential in good as well as hard times.

We need clarity in order for this unique relationship to work for us, so let's establish how the epistolary style works. Epistolary writing dates back to the 13th century as a form of literature whereupon the story develops through written correspondence. I will share something of significance from my life and ask that you respond with whatever reaction befits you, and this will become *our* story line. In a sense, we will be pen pals.

My perception of the world is that very few of us want to feel alone or misunderstood, so if I have piqued your curiosity, then together we will develop a *conversation* sharing important events from our lives. I do hope to offer you something significant as it is my tendency to gravitate toward powerful ideas, and my sense is that you do too. While reading memoirs such *as Eat, Pray, Love* by Elizabeth Gilbert, *The Glass Castle* by Jeanette Wells, and *Wild* by Sheryl Strayed, I know I experienced a very profound connection with the authors. Although their circumstances were unique and personal, I was able to relate to so much of what they shared, and this 'conversation' I began with them, enabled me to resolve some decisions with which I had been grappling. Their revelations had verified that I wasn't alone in regards to the way I felt at certain times; unbeknownst to them, these authors turned out to be kindred spirits for me. They weren't actively seeking a response as I am asking of you, yet I felt a strong desire to continue my connection in some manner. Their direct, at times painfully honest memoirs don't ask anyone to approve or disapprove of their lifestyle or the events which shaped them, but I found myself longing to sit down with them over a glass of wine to talk some things through. It struck me that although I am not well known or famous, it is the everywoman in me that wants to reach out and connect. Perhaps some of my fragments can offer you the same sense of familiarity. You may be waiting to share thoughts and ideas too but haven't found your outlet yet. Maybe this can be your outlet, for it may well be cathartic for you to share in the events of another who has laughed and struggled at times as a girl, woman, mother, wife, sister, daughter, employee, or child of the universe. The fact is *your* existence *has* given me strength; you have given me power to beat some of my demons simply because you are out there working at yours. I hope as I offer some of the fragments which have shaped me, you will nod acknowledging that you were not living in isolation in certain situations. As the Feng Shui architect R. D. Chin states, "This is why it helps to share our journey with others, because in doing so we become a chorus of voices, and the stress of going solo lessens once we discover that we are not alone." As you are for me, I am here for you sharing the same journey as a kindred spirit. I hope that matters as much to you as it does to me.

Because I intend for this to be a true epistolary experience for us, there will be pages provided for you after each chapter in order to record your thoughts and reactions. You may share your thoughts on any or all chapters with me at eballman72@gmail.com, where you may also access my blog. It may take a while, but I promise to respond to you and *your* shared fragments. As you read, you may consider making notes in the margins, highlighting similarities, earmarking in order to return later, or underlining a specific connection. Do it now if you want, so you can react in the moment, or return to it later. Reflection is one of our greatest gifts, and hindsight's gift allows us to look at situations through wiser eyes. Together I want us to use these gifts in order to make sense of the fragments of our lives.

Reflection #1: Write about a time when you have needed to believe that someone in the universe understood what you were feeling. Write about times that even your closest friends or partners don't know about because you felt they couldn't understand or relate. I am sure you will want to share a tough time, but please also share a joyous time because as strange as it seems, we aren't always able to freely share certain joys. Free write and find *your* voice while shooting for total honesty; no one has to read this, unless you want me to.

(Entry#1) Several pages follow for your journaling.

My Thoughts and Reactions

Chapter 1
Character Traits

Hopefully, by the time we have shared this first fragment you will have a better sense of how this will work and what I hope we can accomplish together. Because these are simply fragments of my life, the topics have come to me in no particular order. If you have a particular interest, you could use the Table of Contents as your guide. Each chapter ends with pages for your reflections.

Like numerous of you, I am a horse of many colors; I have done all kinds of different jobs to earn a living, I have worked all over the country, and I have met a wide variety of people at those jobs. Some jobs I have loved, while others I basically persevered or hung on until I could replace it. I have met some exceptional people on my work journey, yet I have also learned quite a lot from those who were not all that inspiring. Because we spend so much of our time with coworkers, would you agree that it is important to consider the impact these relationships have on our lives? What are the qualities which earn your respect and draw you towards establishing a connection beyond a simple nod; which character traits do you find yourself attracted to? What are the turn-off traits causing you to avoid certain people? Maybe take a moment to jot down some of these traits and characteristics while they are fresh and then rejoin me.

Now that you are warmed up, I am going to ask you to make a list of some of *your* qualities and character traits, the ones which others may find attractive or possibly even off-putting. Make a comprehensive list and be honest. When the list is long and inclusive, it feels satisfying, doesn't it? Well, now comes the harder part of this thought process because what if after all was said and done, you were asked to limit yourself to two or three traits which you believed defined you? Furthermore, what if a career depended on your ability to decide which two character traits made you the perfect candidate? Could you do it? Well, I was asked to do just such a thing, and it was a very insightful and revealing exercise and one I believe you are going to enjoy. Here are the circumstances and the results of this assessment.

I felt a strong *calling* to become a high school English teacher, and it was the decision to enter the field of teaching which brought me to these circumstances. I need to give you a wee bit of background for this to make sense, so hear me out. In order to achieve this calling, I would have to return to school and start from scratch as my past degrees and experiences weren't usable credits, yet I wholeheartedly accepted it was worth whatever was required of me. Happily for me, from day one I loved my return to academics, and I gave myself fully to my classes at the women's college I attended, Salem College in Winston Salem, NC. School felt right from the first; it fit me like a glove. What a gift this proved to be at this time in life, and I would like to acknowledge that I knew it and appreciated it right from the start. Do you understand what I mean about an experience that feels so validating? Perhaps you are able to relate to something bold you have done to change your own lives. If so, then I need say no more. If you don't relate yet, no worries because life is long and fluid and bold moves may be yet to come. This college experience was one of the best times of my life, yet as you can imagine, it was also a challenging time. I was a mother of two young sons and by returning to school, I reduced our family's income quite a bit, limited our social life due to studies, and our family time revolved around my workload. Everyone paid a bit of a price while I pursued my dream, but the support was there, and in the end it was absolutely worth the struggle as well as the mounting student loans. For me, becoming a teacher has been second only to being my sons Jake and Josh's mother. Actually, volunteering in my son's classrooms was the catalyst for this life change as the exposure to their many wonderful teachers played a pivotal role in my decision. Hopefully, watching me work so hard for something will rub off on my sons one day. But, you may wonder, why does she digress? Why isn't she talking about those character traits? Thanks for your patience, dear reader. I am about to get there.

In 2004, I was a graduate with a Bachelor's Degree in English, working on my Licensure for teaching, and filled with a nervous energy and excitement; I felt well prepared to begin this new career and all I needed was that first break. I was told that when interviewing for teaching positions, it was common practice to be asked to offer up two or three character traits that 'defined' you. Perhaps it was the current interviewing style, and things may have changed since, but it turned out to be an excellent exercise and one from which I gained valuable insight. Luckily having been alerted to this interviewing technique, I had time to reflect and prepare. It proved a more demanding task than I had anticipated, but once begun, it offered an introspection that was quite rewarding. I did feel the need to be completely honest with myself in the process, yet I was also pretty sure that there were certain traits that a principal would expect applicants to comfortably assign themselves. Thinking about how to best approach this, I decided to use order and method, and I hope you will do so also. Almost all of us at one time or another, has been encouraged to make the pros and cons list, and this list idea presented itself as the perfect beginning. I could flesh out the big ideas after I got the main traits down and hopefully this process could then be whittled to the necessary two or three. The pros came quickly and you may imagine I shunned my cons, but honesty requires you face down your negative qualities too and frankly we all have a few. This self-analysis proved to be thought provoking and worthy of my time, interview or not, and one you will find enlightening. Read on to see where this exercise led me, and see if you can find a part of yourself in my list; I have a feeling you will find a few traits we share.

I am a dreamer and a bit of a Pollyanna. I am open-minded and rarely judgmental. I am unbelievably strong, yet I am extremely gullible. I am compassionate. I am the devil's advocate when needed. I am fair. I am my own worst enemy at times. I am wise, funny, smart, and positive. I throw up walls and cut off my nose to spite my own face at times. I worry about things I can't change. I don't like to ask for help. I am a bit dramatic, very determined, and a bit controlling. Nature is my muse and savior. I am an environmentalist. I am grateful for what I have, but I am not complacent. I am excited and social. I am vain. I am fit. I like to be alone at times, but I fear loneliness. I am patient when it is needed. I am passionate. I have integrity. I am honest. I believe in everyone, and I believe in me. I can be outspoken. I am a good friend. I am a good mother. I am a good listener. I have been a good but difficult wife. I am a hard worker. I do not quit. I am respectful. I am curious. I am a feminist. I am a good person.

This list reflects the *me* I know very well, yet I am sure others would add or subtract from it given the chance. I sit and look over the list; the list stares back. I sit and re-read, edit, add, and I realize it is going to be extremely difficult to choose only two qualities. I have a story for each quality or truth that I have written here and this only adds to my difficulty. Here is the thing, though; you don't always get to tell all of your stories. In this instance, what describes you in a nutshell is what matters; that is your task. Here is what I said, and I continue to believe that these two qualities make me an excellent teacher, friend, and human. In my interview, I told this principal that I was first and foremost compassionate and passionate.

I cannot envision a classroom where these won't be the most important traits. I don't believe it is limited to classrooms, but if you are a parent and have lived through the school experience, I think you would agree that what your child needs more of in school is compassion and passion. These traits may seem redundant, but they are indeed very unique qualities. Listen to my reasoning on this to see if you can agree.

Compassionate means that for each student walking through your door, you pledge to try to see the world through his or her eyes before you make any decision regarding your interactions with him or her. Atticus Finch in *To Kill a Mockingbird* gave the most profound advice about being compassionate to his confused daughter, Scout. In order to help her understand folks, he offered these words, "First of all," he said, "if you can learn a simple trick, Scout, you'll get along a lot better with all kinds of folks. You never really understand a person until you consider things from his point of view…until you climb into his skin and walk around in it (Lippincott 36)." In other words, you need to ask yourself why this person is acting the way he or she is; what might be happening in his or her personal life? Are things OK at home? Is he or she being bullied, did they fail a test in another class, did they just break up with a first love? If you feel compassionate toward people, you will allow yourself time to take inventory first and then deal with the situation in the correct manner. This trait is not only necessary for your students, but your peers, the administrators, the support staff, and any member of the 'village' that is a school environment. It is needed for your neighbors, the grocery clerk, waiter or waitress, or the librarian. It is not always easy, but if you make it your priority to act compassionately, you can change the dynamics of any given situation. If you believe it is important, it will begin to come naturally, and you will always be the solution and not add to the problem. Yes, compassion has made my life more difficult. It takes time and patience to get to the root of what ails others, but I promise you, walking in their skin offers a better solution than rash, unsuitable behavior in the moment.

You may well ask why the character trait passionate is so unlike compassionate. Here is why: Passion for your subject is imperative if you expect to deliver it successfully. Think about it; do you love what you do? Is it joyful to spend your time endeavoring to excel at your craft? Do you think about it continuously simply because it is as easy as breathing to immerse yourself in thoughts on the topic? Then you know passion. I had a professor in college, Dr. Mowbry, who by my measure set the standard of passion. He taught an ornithology class recommended by the dean as a way of fulfilling a science lab requirement. I was trying hard to get my degree in the shortest amount of time, and he taught a lab class on Saturdays that would work. Truth is, I took it to check a box and move on. I dreaded the Saturday aspect of it as it cut into the time I had with the boys on weekends. Yes, I will be honest, it cut into my Friday night fun too as I had to be out the door fresh for a 4 hour class each Saturday morning while others got to dilly-dally as one should on a weekend. Remember, I claimed social as one of my traits, but I also said I am determined, wise, and smart, so off to class I went. It only took that first class to see I was in for a treat. This was not to be a dull lecture and an hour at the end with binoculars, not at all. Dr. Mowbry loved the study of ornithology, and he made me love it too. He would speak eloquently about his subject, and at times he would get so intent on making his point that he would end up on his toes, with his entire body leaning forward as he expressed how important each little detail of a bird's wing was to its flight capabilities. Seriously, you found yourself leaning toward him at the front of the lecture hall, hanging on the details, picturing the bone structure, grateful to glean a bit of his vast knowledge. Let me add here that because of his passion, he was a demanding teacher, and it was an extremely difficult class with one of the most brain draining exams I have ever endured. But what else would you expect from someone passionate? His talent as an instructor exemplified what teaching could be, and I knew I wanted to bring that passion into my classroom. I grasped the significance a passionate delivery becomes as justification for reading Steinbeck, Shakespeare, Chaucer, Shelley, and as many other iconic authors as we can cram into our semester because I, myself, experienced it firsthand. Later, hearing my own students say they loved an assigned novel was reward beyond any salary a teacher receives because my passion had hooked them and reeled them in. Sadly, I never told Dr. Mowbry how much I learned from him. I know I wrote a wonderful assessment of his class as I exited at the spring's end, but it would have been far better to have told him in person. Let me finish up by sharing one last point about this extraordinary class. One of our semester-long assignments was keeping a journal documenting the birds we saw on our own time. We had to seek out birds in a variety of settings and give the details and characteristics of the bird, as well as when and where we spotted it. Remember, certain birds return to areas at specific times, so you best not try to get one over on him as he would surely know if you were faking your journal entry. I not only adhered to the regiment and integrity of the journal, but I did my best to excel at it. I wanted him to know that I was giving it my all out of respect for him. That is what passion does; it makes others want to achieve a level of excellence in homage to yours. I valued his comments on my entries and the A I got on the project was a testament to how his great passion had affected me. How lucky I was, and still am, to have been exposed to such a passionate man.

A few last thoughts on passion: In Sarah Ban Breathnach's best-seller *Simple Abundance*, she offers her thoughts on passion. "What we don't realize is that passion is the muse of authenticity. It's the primordial, pulsating energy that infuses all of life, the numinous presence made known with every beat of our hearts (Grand Central Publishing 2009)." I think this sums up passion beautifully, and I hope you will agree that this should be an important quality for all of us. If it is not on your list, please reflect on its significance and perhaps try to find room for it on your life journey.

Deciding on two or three character traits which define you is your assignment. Will you do it? Maybe if you can think about it this way it may help. When we were kids, our father used to ask one thing of us, and it was simply this: "Be a good person." We rolled our eyes and laughed at his simplistic directive, but as I got older I began to see the wisdom of reducing things to their simplest form. He could have told us many specific things to strive for, and we would have rolled our eyes some more, but 'being a good person' in the end is about the best that can be said of you. Instead of making things so complex, try to simplify when you can. If you take the challenge of finding two traits, understand that in order to simplify, you must first explore all the options. You can start by highlighting or circling ones you share in my list of traits. (See the teacher in me here?) Then, of course, think about your own stories and add to the list. After editing, come back and circle the two or three qualities or traits that define you. Think about the history behind your selections as I have just done, and write to me about it in the journal. Pretend it's for your epithet and imagine how peers, friends, and family will smile because they will agree and find peace in the words inscribed which defined the essence of the *you* they knew and loved.

(Entry#2) Several pages follow for your journaling.

My Thoughts and Reactions

_____

_____

_____

_____

_____

_____

_____

_____

_____

_____

_____

_____

_____

_____

_____

_____

_____

_____

_____

_____

_____

Chapter 2
Family Bonds

At this point it seems the natural progression is to talk with you a bit about the people who played a principle role in my formative years. Maybe after meeting them, you will see where a few of those character traits we discussed in Chapter 1 were established. Although I am now a far cry from the young girl they called Leenie, impressions of my childhood prevail as important steppingstones toward my adult makeup. I think you will enjoy these impressions of my family, and I hope for most of you it will stir up fond memories of yours. Because we are simply sharing fragments, I will only tap the surface, but you will get the gist.

I was fortunate enough to have had an exceptional childhood. Yes, I do refer to the kind where there was plenty of running, racing, game playing, security, and love. Sure, some specifics are murky as it is difficult to separate which is family lore or which are my own recollections before a certain age, yet my impression of being a happy child is well founded. Family stories and legends do seem to bear this out. I am from a large, Irish Catholic family of eight kids. There are four girls and four boys with me smack in the middle as the fifth to arrive. This was great with me and I liked my position because I could play with my younger brothers on any given day, and my older sisters let me join in with them on others. We lived in a large, kid-filled neighborhood but if no friends were around, I had plenty of siblings who let me into their respective worlds.

When you are from a large family, it is easy to get lost in the family dynamics and day-to-day drama. As you would imagine, I wasn't very close to my older brothers, John and Micky, because they were six and seven years older than me, and there was absolutely no reason for me to be on their radar. What I do remember, though, is them getting into all kinds of trouble with some of their friends. I remember my dad going to bail them out of jail for teenage boy hijinks: driving too fast, drinking beer, rabble rousing, and taunting the local cops. I also recall I had a crush or two on their handsome friends; one in particular was John's friend Bob. He parted his hair on the side and all of that thick black hair sort of swooped out over his forehead and then drooped just so over his dark eyes. Lord, he was movie star material. I left him a valentine once, and he was kind enough not to tease me. My brother Micky was extremely good looking himself with a charismatic charm that attracted girls of all ages. He was a bit of a rogue and even charmed the mothers of the girls he went out with because he really was hard to resist. His eyes were deep hazel and sparkled with mischief; he had thick reddish brown hair he wore too long and arching brows over a strong Roman nose. Many of my friends had crushes on him, and we stalked him a bit for their benefit. John was good-looking in a less dramatic fashion; he used Brill Cream in his strawberry blond hair and had impossibly blue eyes and fair, freckled skin. He had a steady girlfriend who worked at the local hamburger hangout. I do recall well the weight of losing them as they were the first to leave home: one was drafted and left to fight as a sniper in Viet Nam and was never again to be quite the same, while the other married that girl from the hamburger shop and become an excellent house painter and wallpaper hanger and carpenter. Years later, I would become more like friends with them both because the years between us wouldn't matter as I too moved into adulthood, but that's another story for another time.

My older sisters, Maureen and Pat, are five and two years older than me respectively. I looked up to Maureen, kind of idolized her actually. She was so pretty with big brown, dreamy eyes and she wore make-up and curled her hair in those large pink plastic rollers, and she dressed in the latest trends when not in her Catholic High uniform. I remember her in tight (pegged) white jeans and a light blue oxford shirt, tied around the waist, of course, and a jaunty flip to her hair; to me she looked glamorous and poised as she walked out the door to meet her friends. Now, as an adult who went through that teenage angst myself where I rarely acknowledged my good points, I realize that she probably felt very differently and would tell that story like this; legs too heavy, chest too flat, hair too thin, a blemish on her chin…but I saw none of that, for she was the one I looked to as a measure of the things I couldn't wait to become. I fantasized about myself when I reached her age; like her, I would wear stockings held up by a garter belt, I would wear a black mantilla in church, and I would walk up to holy communion wearing those red patent leather heels that clicked and tapped as she walked up the granite aisle. I would 'like' boys and stay up late and pierce my ears. I would put Summer Blonde in my hair, and I would join the Fife and Drum Corp and twirl a flag in white boots. She really seemed like a movie star to a younger, impressionable me, and the fact that she actually allowed me a tiny space in her exotic lifestyle felt like a gift then. Yes, she did torture me at times too as older sisters do, but such was the price one paid for the 'heady' experiences that were bestowed on me when she was feeling generous.

My sister Pat was an entirely different person, and I counted on her stability. Pat was infamous in our family because she was so smart. She started school early and then skipped a grade so she graduated younger than her classmates at the ripe old age of 16. This meant she was always with older kids, and perhaps that explains why she was 'older' than her years in many respects. I was born on her second birthday and we are Gemini twins in every sense of the word. She is shorter, has dark hair, hazel eyes, and is more conservative and cautious. I am taller, blue-eyed, liberal, and like to throw myself out into situations. There is, however, an unmistakable bond between us that is more real and down to earth than any physical differences. We have always been able to talk and share our ups and downs, and we have never been estranged as I have been with Maureen and my younger sister Nancy. Of anyone in my family, I can, and have, counted on Pat. Maybe you can get a better sense of her if I tell you something that I discovered many years past our childhood. The oldest three were pretty wild. It was the 1960s and they embraced the rebellious behavior of their generation. Pat, however, didn't cause my parents problems and stayed out of the fray for the most part, and we thought of her as a bit dull compared to what was happening in our society. I mean she did sneak cigarettes and drink a beer, but she was not blatant about any of it. Later, she told me that she just couldn't add to our parents' hell because they were so overwhelmed with the older one's exploits while trying to raise the rest of us. Maybe I was too young or self-centered to notice my parents' stress level, truthfully after 6th grade, I added to it, but she saw it and consciously determined she would not create more misery for them. I give her the credit she deserves, for I am sure she had some tough days and wished to simply cut loose too, but she did her best not to add to what was already a struggling marriage. Although I hero-worshipped my older sister Maureen, it was for the glitz and glam. Hindsight shows it was Pat who offered the better road map. But, this journey with you is about trying to see who I was then in order to understand who I became, and I am simply looking for the history that evolved me into the person of today. I accept hindsight and reflection as the gifts they are, and I want to be careful reviewing the past lest I begin regretting every wrong decision or mistake rather than celebrating my life.

I have come to my place in the family order, and so I will simply tell you that I was a small, skinny girl with big blue eyes and dishwater blonde hair. I had tons of freckles, and I thought of myself as a tomboy who sported scabs rather than girly bows. When I was five, I fell off a large construction dirt mound in our neighborhood and fractured my skull. My poor mother waited by my hospital bedside to discover the result of the fall. Can you imagine her worry? Can you imagine her relief when I opened my eyes and knew her? I was going to be fine, which must have been a huge relief with six others at home and two of them under five. Two years later, riding no hands down a hill, I fell off my bike and got a concussion; I am pretty sure this is when I decided to become more cautious in action and deed. To this day, I am not a risk taker on the water, on the slopes, or in the mountains.

I am told I was a sweet and gullible girl. My sister Maureen likes to tell the story of us watching the movie *Peter Pan*, and when we are supposed to clap to save Tinkerbell, it brought me to tears that the older ones wouldn't clap for Tink. The *Sound of Music* was/is my favorite movie, and I still get that lump in my throat when Captain von Trapp sings *Edelweiss*. I wanted to go to heaven where I might get a pony because that is how I imagined the god I learned about in afterschool CCD would reward me; I liked to read all kinds of books, watch Saturday morning TV, ride my bike, and walk our baby sister with my older sisters; I felt right at home in my big, noisy diverse family, so when I went away to my first overnight Girl Scout camp, I wrote letters home telling them how much I missed them, and asked if they missed me. Up until 6th grade, I was a decent enough student and my report cards said in the comments that I was maybe a bit too talkative. Let me add now that I am sure if this was one of my sibling's memoirs describing me, things would be remembered differently as they were either older or younger with their own perspectives, but I honestly recall the child I am describing. I also remember when I began to change from the sweet, young girl I just depicted and began the descent into selfish teen, but that is definitely for another time.

I won't do this often, but I want to digress for a moment and add the only negative result of coming from a large family. I discovered later on in life that when alone, I had a real fear of the dark. We three older girls slept together in a large bedroom, and if you have grown up drifting off to the rise and fall of your sisters' breathing, to the sound of their tossing and turning, and to the ever present smell of your sisters' blemish cream, Avon's Skin So Clear, it becomes extremely difficult to find peace in the dead quiet after they have grown up and moved away. When alone, I discovered that I had a vivid imagination, one which would take flight and run wild at the simplest sounds; never mind that my clothes, seen through the closet door crack, you know the one that won't ever completely shut no matter how you try, would become creepy, old, raggedy men who frightened me. On a hot summer night I daren't throw my leg over the side of the bed anymore because the 'monster' living under it would surely grab me and pull me into its lair. No, it is not a stellar time in one's life to discover you are a 'fraidy cat'. I am 62 years old now, and I have finally conquered this fear I am happy to say, but my 20s, 30s, 40s, and some of my 50s were years fraught with fears and nights spent with the lights blazing. When my husband, Dave, was on the road, which was often as he was a sales rep, I would set the TV timer for 2 hours after getting into bed at night in the hopes I would be asleep long before it turned itself off and that 'click' become the boogey man trying to get in my bedroom. Yes, it appears childhood routines do shape the adults we become in many different ways, right down to adult fears.

Okay, digression time is over but I would hope you will hang tough with me if I digress again throughout this memoir, for at times it just starts to flow as does a stream of consciousness…much like it would if we were sitting over a cup of tea or a glass of wine, and I know you would have had a story to match mine, right? Definitely write me about it. For now, though, back to rest of the clan.

My younger brothers Mark and Jim are closer in age, so I spent much more time with them than my older brothers. These two younger brothers were pure entertainment. They made you smile just looking at them. Man, they were so cute. They were all freckles and huge blue eyes with terrible haircuts that included the infamous 'white sidewalls' of the late '50s and early '60s. Simply observing them, it became evident that they were having that ideal childhood. You know the one we discussed where they ran, raced, laughed, and played the days away. Mark and Jim, for that is how you spoke of them, as if they were one, not Mark or Jim, Mark and Jim, were what we called 'pips'. We lived in a sprawling neighborhood where kids played outside all day and drank from the hose when they needed to be refreshed. Mothers kept an eye on all of the kids who gathered in their yards, at least until we moved en masse to the next diversion in someone else's yard, field, or street corner, when some other mother now took up sentry duty. We showed up at our own houses for a quick lunch of PBJ's or bologna and cheese when hungry and then back out the door we went. Red Light/Green Light, Red Rover, Hide and Seek, and Tag were played throughout the nice days and card games like Go Fish, Old Maid, and Rummy or board games like Risk, Monopoly, and Parcheesi in basements or playrooms on rainy days. When not with my sisters or girlfriends, I happily played with Mark and Jim, joining in on such entertainment as young boys would find. When allowed, my favorite game was playing *Combat* with them. Many of you will remember that TV show which was so popular in the '60s. Vic Morrow led his men on combat missions and we loved reenacting them. They, of course, expected the girls to be nurses, but I longed to be Cage, the handsome, sexy French character with the 5'o clock shadow. I couldn't see why I had to be relegated to female roles even back then. I don't think I overtly rebelled, but I definitely questioned a world where because you were male, you got to decide things without at least a discussion. I was a tomboy and I could run as fast as any boy and I had the Field Day ribbons to prove it; I am sure I felt equal to any challenge that a combat mission could offer. However, some of Mark and Jim's other entertainments were better avoided. For instance, Mark and Jim decided to trap muskrats and make a coat to give to our mother. They did manage to trap one and had to skin it and stake the skin to a board to dry...disgusting. They also liked to fish, but worms and hooks were not for me; they jumped off rope swings into ponds full of frogs and snakes. No thanks! We all learned to ski in our backyard, but they were both outstanding skiers, and I couldn't begin to keep up with them on their hair-raising runs; they were a sight in their fearless assault of the slopes.

As happens, the days of Mark and Jim wound down, and eventually they grew apart. I had started middle school and things changed completely for me. I no longer wanted to run the streets with them, and they began hanging with their own school friends. Mark and our neighbor the other Mark became the deadly duo, and as he advanced in school, he made some new friends and went his own way. Jim found some kids that he enjoyed being with much more than Mark's sort of preppy guys, and the days of Mark and Jim ended. There was one last thing, however, that continued to bond them while at home, and that was torturing our baby sister Nancy.

I told you I am the middle child in this large, complex family. I am married to the eldest in his family and after listening to him, I am glad that wasn't my lot. Too many expectations of the oldest, being lost in the middle was just fine with me. As for being the youngest, well I am pretty sure I wouldn't want that for myself either, for I like having experienced the many years amongst my numerous siblings. As the youngest, Nancy is 16 years younger than John. How can they even have any childhood memories? They can't, though happily Nancy has that with the younger of us. As adults, we are all over the place as far as personalities and lifestyles go, but when you gather over a holiday table, inevitably you revert to childhood stories. As the baby, she enjoyed many privileges, but she also endured being the last man out at times. Maybe that is why the torture from Mark and Jim stands out as such an important incident in our life.

It is proof she participated in the legend of us Conley kids, and we sure laugh at gatherings as we recall the story.

There was a tale going around that many of you may remember from the late '60s, but if not, you know of some other urban legend meant to frighten. One of ours was the story of the man with 'the golden arm'. It was creepy and scary and if told in the dark of night, could scare the bejesus out of you. Of course the boys told the story to Nancy and from then on, any chance they got to scare her about this man walking the earth wailing, "Who stole my golden arm?", they would. There were countless things they did to harass her; I doubt she had much peace at all, though as is typical of most siblings, it was done out of a sort of innocent fun. Torture is just what happens in families. Maybe it makes you a tougher person for surviving it? I was just enough older than the boys that I didn't partake in this form of family affection with them, but I had plenty of interactions with Nancy to look back on.

I was 9 years old when she was born, and I remember it felt like I had a real live doll with which to play. She was adorable from the start, though she did have this very fine kind of crazy hair with a cowlick, however, my mother, who was prone to pixie haircuts for ease with girls, simply carried on the tradition she had begun with us older girls and took care of that. I confess none of us three older girls carried off that pixie look like this little doll did.

When I was 18, our parents divorced. Nancy was only 9 years old and pretty confused about the fact that my father moved out of our childhood home and clearly wasn't coming back. It was a difficult time for my mother, of course, and I thought I was being a good sister/daughter by stepping in and including Nancy and her friends a bit more in my life. Here is the not-so-great part of my plan; I did not curtail my lifestyle when including her on these outings. My friends and I carried on with few thoughts as to what we were exposing Nancy and her friends to. We smoked cigarettes and pot, and we drank our quarts of Schlitz, and we piled into cars to head to the beaches or to state park campgrounds with the kids in tow. Looking back on it now, I feel a sense of embarrassment and, of course, remorse. She shouldn't have been exposed to that behavior so young, and it was totally irresponsible of me. I could have done a better job of paying attention to her in more appropriate ways. I should have prepared her for teenage angst, weird guys, girl drama, or how to survive the family dysfunction brought about by divorce. Oh, I did do a few things that she thinks were cool. I filled in as her room mother when our mother couldn't and went on a few field trips with her class; she mentions that was a highlight for her. Apparently it added to her status a bit to have a more hip person on these trips. But the truth is, when there are 9 years between you, it is very hard to have a meaningful relationship. Later in life, when I had finally matured enough to be the kind of sister I thought she needed, she didn't want that kind of advice from me and some harsh words were exchanged and caused a rift that took us a while to move past. You see, I was trying to save her from what I perceived were bad choices, such as the very partying I had done at her age. Can you just imagine her outrage at this kind of counseling from someone who for as long as she could remember had done exactly what she was being chastised for? No, thank you, sister, mind your own business. If I could change anything about my past, I would change what I exposed Nancy and her friends to during those years, although I don't regret the bond we had at the time for it wasn't all bad. We did some entertaining things just for diversion's sake, and I was able to connect with her at that level. Weirdly enough, being on each other's radars was worth it for me. My father once told me something profound when I was struggling with some choices my son Jake was making at the time, and it has helped me often over the years. He said, "You can't put your older head on a younger person's shoulders." How wise, right? In the end, Nancy has grown up to be quite a smart, beautiful woman, and I am sure she looks back at many things in her life with regrets, but they are hers to regret as my regrets are mine. As I mentioned earlier, be careful when reminiscing and journaling. Cut yourself some slack while you reflect, for today's clarity is due to yesterday's mistakes.

There is so much to say about family, and this smattering of events doesn't come close to revealing my childhood. Yet, I hope you hear the *voice* behind the words, and I hope you take the time now at this chapter's end to think back on your family dynamics. Relive some of your better moments, or if you have a demon or two regarding family, let them out now. As you suspect from reading between the lines, writing these fragments about my family has been enjoyable and cathartic for me. Next time you gather with your brothers and sisters, be sure to laugh about childhood memories and forget about your adult differences. When my mother died and we all gathered to celebrate her life, we spent many hours together cleaning out her small apartment. Each thing we touched had a story, and we had so much to share from our childhood days. From the oldest to the youngest we laughed a lot, and that was the best way we could honor our mom who kept her diverse children a family long after we left to become our individual selves.

On the next pages, write about your family members and share a few vivid memories about your childhood with me. If you were an only child, write about how that felt, for I have no way to know unless you tell me. Did you make your friends your family? Did you love having all of the focus and attention? I so wish we were gathered around a table right now, for I would absolutely love to hear what you have to say about your childhood bonds.

Entry #3 follows

My Thoughts and Reactions

_____

_____

_____

_____

_____

_____

_____

_____

_____

_____

_____

_____

_____

_____

_____

_____

_____

_____

_____

_____

_____

Chapter 3
Loss of Innocence

If you had the chance to do some things over, do you think you would jump at the opportunity? If possible, would you travel back to specific events from your past in order to rewrite them? What if you could return to your younger teen self with today's wisdom, is that an enticing notion? I guess the substantive question for you is this: Would you wish for a 'do-over' of some painful past events? Over the years I listened while friends shared tales of the demons still chasing them, particularly ones from their youth. My impulse was, and still is, to advise them to leave it alone and let bygones be bygones; leave those demons behind you and focus on the present. Yet, ironically, I find myself here about to share some of the things which still have the power to haunt me. Maybe this ruminating is a necessary step in a healing process, and I now find myself speculating about what advice you may offer me. Will your counsel be to simply let it all go? I also wonder what bee's nests I will have stirred as you contemplate your own teenage history and the loss of innocence, for it seems it typically occurs during those years. Indulge me as I invite you into a part of my naïve past and the impact loss of innocence had on me. Then perhaps you can help me decide if it is a history I would rewrite or not.

Both men and women alike find themselves sharing experiences from their early teens, and for most this reverie instantly conjures up feelings of awkwardness and insecurity. For instance, my husband Dave shot up in his teens but wasn't able to put on a pound no matter how many baloney sandwiches he ate. He vividly recalls what it felt like to be too tall and too skinny and how his peers teased him. His nickname at school was *bird* and when he recounts this, it is clear how much this affected his sense of self-confidence at this time. Frankly, I found his admission intriguing because I will admit I never did give much thought as to how boys may have been feeling because I myself was so self-conscious in front of them. You see, boys added to my teenage misery; therefore, I never saw the need to empathize on their behalf. Not to digress again so soon, but I would like to state here and now that as the mother of sons and also as a high school teacher, I called upon the difficult lessons of my own youth at times, but I also kept Dave's revelations in mind. The fact is that teen years for boys and girls can be extremely difficult, and I watched each gender with equal concern. This revelation comes from my own experience as well as listening to others sharing and that seems like a point in case for **not** returning to a past to rewrite your history doesn't it? After all, experience has proven to be our best teacher.

Remember earlier on I talked with you about a childhood where my being a tomboy kind of girl was an excellent and satisfying life. Up until around 12 years old, I was living a carefree, happy existence, but as can happen when least expected, life has a way of getting all lopsided on you. Without warning you unwittingly age out of what had once been accepted behaviors, and prepared or not, you find yourself thrown into the unknown. That is exactly what happened with me.

Around age twelve, I began to notice several significant changes occurring with my girlfriends; this was the natural maturing process of most girls in this age group; they were beginning to develop curves and bumps and this natural phenomenon was about to change everything. Their conversations began to change as they talked about 'pads' and bra size and pimples; they were miserable with 'cramps' during 'that time of the month'. Of course I had heard all about this stuff in a 6th grade health class; we were paraded to the auditorium where we endured a video that showed the sloughing off of blood each month and how we were to deal with it. They sent us home with pamphlets which said that when this happened to you, you were now a woman. Some called this monthly occurrence the 'curse', and my older sisters said things like "Alice is in town". I recall that no one made any part of it sound like a good thing, so I was content, or so I thought, to avoid this woman thing for years to come. I should be happy that my body wasn't changing yet, right? Think about it, I wasn't enduring all this physical misery, yet ironically in being left out of this woman thing I began to suffer from something that felt just as painful in its own right. I was becoming an outsider amongst my best friends. I wasn't able to be a part of the conversation.

I will paint a scenario that some of you may have endured at one time or another. It is time to shop for a bathing suit, and my friends are getting cute bikinis or two-piece suits in the Woman's Department. These suits have bras built in and my friends have developed nice, firm breasts which fill these cups out perfectly. They have a waist and rounded hips and they look fantastic. I, on the other hand, have absolutely no breasts yet, none. My suit cups are empty, so the bra cups lay there misshapen and puckered on this boney chest. My waist is the same size as my hips so no nice curves, and as I look in the mirror, I know that I look ridiculous in the same suits in which my friends look like *Seventeen Magazine* models. What do I do, go back to the little girls department to find a bikini with no bra built in? Should I wear a swim team type one-piece suit? Lord, then everyone would know I was built like a little boy, not to mention, I wasn't on a swim team, and thus begins a time of self-consciousness that will stay with me for years to come. I think the worst part must have been that I felt I couldn't talk with anyone about this lack of development. I loved my mother, but she was a no nonsense woman, and she wasn't going to take this awkwardness seriously and I sensed that. She had this saying that covered traumas, "This too shall pass," and later in life it was a proven truth, but right now, I needed a different kind of wisdom. I wonder if my sisters would have advised me if I had been able to talk to them about it, but they had long since developed themselves, and I felt they wouldn't understand. Heck, this misery may even have been grounds for sister torture if I had told them. Would my friends have sympathized if I had had the nerve to talk about any of this with them? I will never know now of course, but perhaps you may want to journal about how you would have helped a struggling me. Take a moment if you want to hang around this idea of maturing. You might also write about how it felt to begin to have curves and bumps yourself and how that may have made you self-conscious or nervous around those teen boys, especially if you developed earlier that your friends and peers. That must have been misery too, or was it amazingly fantastic to sense the power this female shape now offered you?

Well, things did not get easier; for it turns out I was going to be a very late bloomer. I survived 6th grade as there were a few other girls built like me. I mentioned previously that I was a fast runner making me a minor star in our Field Day events that year, and this definitely helped my self-esteem. But middle school loomed and I had already heard tales of mature girls and boys walking the halls and holding hands and dating and making out; I instinctively felt it was going to get harder and harder to feel like I fit into this exotic new world looking as I did. I was set to attend the small Catholic middle school associated with our parish, which may have felt a wee bit less intimidating until reality set in. As you know, life in parochial school requires wearing a white blouse as part of the uniform, and though I did not really need a bra, I knew I had to have one showing through that white blouse or risk being teased or ridiculed. My mother did seem to understand this so off we went to the department store to take care of it. Those bras fit like the bathing suits had, and friends it is a sad thing to have a trainer bra wrinkled and puckered where soft flesh should be filling it out. It was humiliating to me, this lack of a female figure, and I became so obsessed that I decided the only thing for me to do was do what nature had not and that was to stuff my bra. I would create breasts and those fake symbols of maturity would open the doorway to that world in which I so desperately yearned to participate.

Well, if you have ever walked a road of deception, fellow readers, you know that it is indeed a treacherous slope. If you have not fully thought through the consequences of bra stuffing, you find yourself constantly running into situations unprepared. For instance, if you have breasts during the day, you need to have them at home at night too. Does this mean you have to sleep in your stuffed bra to keep your sisters unaware of what you are up to? It started out just wanting to fit in at school and with girlfriends, but the reality is such that your deception becomes an all-consuming distraction with pitfalls at every turn. You believe you can deceive people, but you have no idea the toll this will take as you try to keep all of the pieces of your deception in play. Here are two examples and two major life lessons for you to ponder and respond to.

If you aren't developing yet, you make the mistake of wearing your stuffed bra too high. Because there is no flesh holding the elastic under the bra cup in place, it tends to rise up and even at times rest on your nipples. You have no sensation there yet, so it can go un-noticed by you, but you will learn that it is not un-noticed by fellow students. Another mistake is that you add the tissues to this bra in order to fill it out, but tissues are not soft and pliant like flesh, therefore, they remain static and immobile while you are in motion. The sad thing is that you do not know the difference because naturally you do not know or understand the weight and motion of a real breast. As I learned later, there are some other aspects of a developing body that I hadn't considered when I plotted to deceive. For instance, hormones can take your pleasant 'playmates' and turn them into crueler creatures than you could have ever imagined. You are not experiencing these mood swings yourself, so you can't get inside the head of someone who is dealing with the changes associated with PMS. Sadly, you don't understand why friends are so great one day and cranky with you the next. Then there is also the whole party experience which is changing in your early teens. Rumors spread quickly through the halls of boys who used to simply want such games as Spin the Bottle, who now wanted to 'run bases' and female bodies became their 'infield'. The girls with those swelling breasts became very popular and dark corners at parties became places where running the bases was on most teen boy's minds. Now, how terrifying is the thought that one of these boys might want to get to first base with you? That just couldn't be because they would only find tissues, and you would become a laughing stock. Adding to my misery and confusion was the fact that I would not do well at these new parties if I dared go at all, and I liked parties, who didn't? See what I am saying about the slippery slope? Some of you may be reading this as one of those who developed early. Perhaps your memories are of the terror of not knowing if the boys really liked you or those new breasts. How did that feel? Were you stressed about attending parties where boys wanted to make out, and though you looked more mature, you weren't ready for any of this yet either? I can see now that your road may have been as scary as mine, but at the time, I simply wanted what you had, a beautifully burgeoning body.

Here is an event that stays with me, and I am asking you to consider if it may not have been as traumatic as I recall.

Middle school days introduced a new social life for many of us. Those were days when you began being invited to other's houses right after school, and in my case when this happened you brought your hang out clothes so as not to ruin your school uniform. Like most of you, I had known my classmates in elementary school well as we lived in the same neighborhoods and had played together for as far back as we could remember, but middle school introduced new kids, and it was exciting to get to go to new neighborhoods and expand your horizons. When two girls, who were already good friends, invited me over to hang out with them one afternoon, I was pretty excited because they seemed to be popular, and that meant I would become more popular too if I was allowed into their clique. Yes, knowing what we do about three is a crowd, some of you may already be worried about where this is going; you may be thinking about the potential for problems already, and you would be correct.

Well, we walked to one of the girls' houses after school, and it was suggested we change in order to do something fun outside, so naturally we headed up to her bedroom. Both girls easily and freely began to change their shirts which, of course, revealed real breasts filling out their bras. One of them, let's call her Ellen, had lovely orange-sized breasts and the other one, let's call her Cathy, had full grapefruits; there was serious, beautiful cleavage here, my friends. I felt their eyes on me as they waited for me to change my shirt, and I quickly realized the magnitude of my bra-stuffing mistake because there was simply no way when I took off my shirt that I was **not** going to be revealed as a fraud. The hardest part was when I realized they seemed to already know that I was a fake, and that this had been their plan all along. Their demeanor and body language had an excitement that seemed out of place for simply changing clothes, and I sensed it. I faltered and cast about for the right thing to do or say and ended up asking for the bathroom and insisted it was because I had to use it so I might as well change in there. I sensed their frustration as it dawned on them that if I changed out of sight, I wouldn't be outed by them today.

The dreadful thing about getting caught in a situation like this is that you simply want to confess and tell the truth, maybe even throw yourself at their mercy, but you know you can't. So you do what most liars do and become defensive about it and suggest, "What did it matter where I changed, and if that is how they wanted to act…" I just knew I wanted to get out of there, and I made up some other lies about needing to get home. I know I was trying not to cry as I walked home alone. It was beyond humiliating to discover that my new 'friends' had conspired to embarrass me. How many others knew or suspected or were talking about me and my stuffed bra? I even started to worry about going home because now I had to question if my mother or sisters or, God forbid, my brothers knew. Should I simply stop stuffing it right now and see if anyone noticed? I was too mortified to ask anyone with sense in their head though, and worse yet, I wasn't sure who to trust with this information. If these girls, who were supposedly new friends, plotted and planned to shame me, how could I trust other kids at school? Up until now, I had never experienced this kind of treatment: I really had been an innocent. Sure, we had mentioned the occasional sibling torture, but this was so different and I was completely out of my league. Here is what I decided on that long walk home: I decided I had come too far to stop now, so I would continue to stuff my bra, I would not go to other's homes after school if I had to change, I would work harder at making my fake breasts look real, and I would avoid any dark corners at parties. No longer as innocent or as naïve as I had been before I started this deception, I still felt I needed to follow through with it. Needless to say, my comprehensive plan put a damper on my 7th grade year, but here is good news to share, soon after this episode I met my best friend, Barbara, and though teen angst continued, she and I became such good friends that I began to trust in girlfriends again. As 7th grade ended, I had high hopes that I would develop over the summer and return to 8th grade with natural flesh filling out my bra which would guarantee my last year of middle school would be joyous and carefree. But hold the phone, it is summer and most of any kid's summer revolved around swimming pools. I still lacked flesh for bathing suit tops and was now faced with the fact that those who might not have known about my bra-stuffing tricks, would soon see a flatter Eileen at the swim club. Looks like summer would not be carefree, for there was a new problem I needed to work through. You recall my mentioning that I stuffed my bra with toilet paper; it was a smart choice because it was always on hand and it was disposed of easily. Yes, by now you see my dilemma, for you know toilet paper will dissolve the moment I enter the pool. Perhaps you are now thinking that it was time to stop this charade, and I believe I desperately wanted off this self-perpetuating roller coaster, yet I still saw no way out. At the time, we belonged to a private swim club as did many of my classmates. I knew that they would look upon my slight, little boy body at that club and put two and two together. I could almost feel the finger pointing and whispering. No, no way was I going to let this happen, so here is what I hit upon which felt quite smart at the time. I decided to change out tissue for fabric scraps which could get wet and remain in place if I swam slowly and got calmly in the water rather than jump in with the old wild abandon. It was going to be a constant strain, but I felt it was the solution that would bridge this summer where surely I would finally develop; even a mosquito size bump would help me out.

I have told you that I met Barbara in my 7th grade year, and she was my best friend. She slept over our house often and was accepted as another member of our large family. Barb came from a family of ten kids, so we were kindred spirits in many ways. As close as we were, unfortunately, I couldn't find the words to confess this deception to her. My lie was all-consuming, and yes, I know that sounds dramatic, but remember I mentioned this is one of my character traits. Hopefully, you agree that the very nature of angst is dramatic in the very sense of the word and are aware that I am not exaggerating. Now, here is my second major event as promised: I risked losing my best friend because I was so consumed with myself and the incorrect assumptions that I would be rejected by her, all due to a lack of breasts. Read on to see how it ends. In our family we had to share asking our non-member friends to come to the pool with us, and we were each allowed to have a guest twice a summer. Naturally, I wanted Barb to come with me. She was thin like me, but she had developed and looked nice in her bikini. I guess if I had thought it through, I would have gotten a one piece that summer which would have held the stuffing in more securely, but I had a cute new bikini like all the other girls and wore this to the pool which was risky to say the least. The day was going so well, I had my best friend with me, and we were laughing and sharing 7th-grade stories and envisioning our 8th grade year with anticipation. It was a very hot day and we were lined up at the pool's edge with the rest of the kids waiting for adult swim to be over. The whistle blows, we look at each other and cannon ball. I rose up out of the water laughing and as I did, the scraps of fabric escaped my bathing suit top. I tried to recover quickly by submerging myself as I stuffed them back in while I scanned to see who may have seen this. It was then that I met Barb's eyes and saw the confusion and surprise…or did I? Was it simply guilt or strain or paranoia on my part? We never spoke of it; I pretended that it had not happened. As an adult, I now know that I could have talked to Barbara about it all, she was that wonderful of a friend, but this knowledge comes from hindsight. I also know that something in me must have cracked that day. It was a few days later that I put my scraps and tissues away for good. Funny, I can't remember what specifically made me 'cry uncle' to Mother Nature the day I threw away those scraps. Maybe it was an epiphany about what was really important; I wish I could say what it was, but I honestly have no memory of the thought process. This decision should have been something momentous that I never forgot, yet I have forgotten my entire thought process on it. Maybe the lesson here is that we tend to remember the decision to do the wrong thing but not the decision to do the right thing. I must have finally gotten a bump in 8th grade, but I was also growing taller and remained skinny and felt awkward and unattractive. I got glasses in 8th grade too, which added to my dissatisfaction with myself. Maybe it never was about breasts; maybe it was just the growing pains all teens experience. What do you think? As you have read through this fragment of my life, have you been able to relate in any way? Take the time before we move on to the next chapter and revisit young teen you. Maybe you have something of significance to forgive your young self for too. Be sure and think about the original question. If you could rewrite your history, would you go back and undo whatever your angst related situation was? I have come to the decision that I wouldn't rewrite mine after all. I think that entire episode has added to my compassionate self, and I would not trade that for anything.

Entry #4 follows

My Thoughts and Reactions

Chapter 4
Learning to Move On

Can we talk for a while about this idea of learning to move on in life? Hopefully, as we progress along life's journey, we come to recognize our past mistakes and transgressions as aides in solving current ones, which, of course, are inevitable. I went from that scrawny girl who felt inadequate due to my physical self, to a person full of potential due to a simple message change. I want to share the catalyst for my moving on, for I know you will agree that it usually takes a *something* for transformation to occur.

The best thing that could have happened to any underdeveloped girl at this time in her life was that the famous super model Twiggy stormed the fashion scene. As Britannica puts it, "Her gamine frame and mod look redefined the industry." She certainly altered the message making it possible for those of us who weren't endowed to strut down the hallways as if we were the beautiful ones. Twiggy was extremely thin and flat chested, she had huge heavily lined and lashed eyes, and wore her hair very short accentuating a long, thin neck. She was on the front page of every fashion magazine, and the statement rang loud and clear that thin was beautiful. Wearing fitted shirts accentuating bony shoulder blades tucked into slim fitting pants was the rage. Oh, those poor girls with the curves and bumps could not achieve this look to save their lives, and I wondered if they felt as awkward as I had when they ruled the world. Ah, such is the life of a teenager, 'in' one moment and 'out' the next. If only it was not so intoxicating to be 'in', right? As if the universe knew this couldn't be the norm forever, the Twiggy modeling days seemed short-lived, and she moved on to acting and singing. Before I knew it, I was back to being a too thin, bespectacled, horsey-haired, awkward teen. The curvaceous cheerleaders returned to rule the roost, and a pale, freckled, blue-eyed, Irish girl with a prominent nose should have been doomed to fail on the social register of high school. But here is where loss of innocence comes to my aide, for I had learned from my bra-stuffing days, and I had gained some confidence from my Twiggy days. Most importantly, I knew I didn't want to return to that sense of low self-esteem again. I had history now, and I would use it to my advantage.

I was in high school from 1969-72. As many of will you recall, our society was changing rapidly and dramatically at this time (For you younger readers and friends, ask your moms or grandmothers, for they will enjoy sharing their stories with you.). There were new, fresh messages of self-worth which were not based solely on looks and fashion sense. People who at one point had had no chance of leadership roles due to gender, race, or religion were offered opportunities previously unheard of. Everything was changing for women, and the words I was hearing from the feminist movement rang true and hit home. Along with this new vision of what women wanted, came this new idea that perhaps we didn't have to look like a Barbie doll to be in or successful. Perhaps glasses shouldn't necessarily make you unattractive, and if you didn't want to roll and set your hair, but rather let it grow long and natural, that was fine too. Jeans and t-shirts were acceptable and you were no longer required to wear matching sweater sets, or tassel loafers, or girdles, or even bras if that was your choice. Women's sports were gaining respect on college campuses, and get this; tall, rangy, thoughtful guys with glasses and mops of curls became heartthrobs. Reading for pleasure and book discussion was popular at parties. Music reflected the changing tide and rang forth with its message almost like poetry from artists such as Simon and Garfunkel, Bob Dylan, Joan Baez, and Gordon Lightfoot. Camping out and hiking became the cool thing to do on weekends. There was less about fighting amongst ourselves and more about the peace movement while thoughtful movies brought all kinds of people together under the same roof in unity.

I observed these changes and felt that I could more easily fit into this world which was so accepting; I felt I was finding my home. You see, I wasn't any more attractive or curvaceous, but it didn't matter because here was a place where looks wasn't your sole objective. I know all of that angst centered on superficial ideals seems such a waste of time and energy now, but when you are young, you have no basis for making mature decisions as to what matters in life. What I realized was that my anxious, uncertain past was meant to be left behind, and a fresh new page to write upon was before me. Who in my shoes wouldn't jump on this bandwagon?

I promise you that because of this movement, these major societal changes, my high school experience was far better than it might have been. There was diversity in the halls of school now, and I found likeminded friends and enjoyed a good social life. I was drawn to girls and boys who wanted a change from the status quo, yet I also managed to have friends in all walks of life. I did have some cheerleader friends, and I had some geeky, intellectual friends too, for you didn't have to be beautiful, clear skinned, or physically attractive to be my friend. You just had to be a decent human being. OK, I will admit that there was one group that I did not connect with; I was not a friend of jocks, for I found that most of them had that superior attitude that turned me off. They, however, had no reason to change as they were still the 'gods' of the halls, and there were plenty of females who wanted to hang off their arms and plenty of guys who would make up their cliques and do their bidding simply to be seen as part of their gang.

Are you reflecting back on your high school years while channeling Bruce Springsteen's *Glory Days* as you read? If you want to pause here and reflect on the friends who made your high school years a successful time, or even a miserable time, go to the end of the chapter and write for a bit. I am about to switch gears on you, and it is perhaps going to be a disturbing read. You see, I can't let you think that all it took was Gloria Steinem and Helen Redy to transform me into this fair-minded young woman who now lived a perfect life. As time rolls on, the headlines of the times change and other influences interrupt our path forward too. Sometimes we are strong and resist what we know is the wrong decision, but at other times we choose, intentionally, to act selfishly and foolishly again.

Let's fast forward to my senior year. It was a restless time for me. I was drinking and smoking pot on a regular basis. I even dabbled in some stronger drugs, but happily never really took to them for long. My grades were at an all-time low. I wasn't planning on going to college the year after graduation, so I began skipping school and wasn't very concerned about the consequences. I foolishly never doubted I would graduate, but by May, I was called into the guidance office to find that I was in real danger of failing. What a shock that was, and I couldn't fathom telling my parents any of this. So, in the month before graduation when most seniors skipped, I had to attend all classes and pass all my quizzes and tests. OK, points for me, I did do what I needed and was rewarded with my cap and gown. I 'walked' and sang our class songs, *In My Life* by the Beatles and the infamous Coke song with all of my peers. I do not remember the valedictorian, but I can tell you where the big after party was. My mother had just had a hysterectomy and was too exhausted to attend my graduation. My parents had split up and I think she was too broken to put forth the energy it took to come to a public gathering in a small town. Everyone knew everyone's business, and it may have been too much to expect of her. My father, who had just moved out of our family home came, but our relationship was so strained that there was no dinner celebration or plans following the ceremony and I headed off to the party not really worrying about how my parents felt. I had by this time started taking advantage of the chaos in our home. I am not proud of this, but it should be something you know about me; I was capable of using people when the chips were down. I took my parents personal pain and used it to my advantage. Somewhere, along the way, I had managed to change from a decent person with a moral code, to one who was self-centered, yes, maybe even depraved at times. I looked for opportunities to get away with as much as possible as I pushed the envelope whenever possible. Where along the way did the change in me take place? Is there one specific day? Of course not, it is a slow process and it starts with making the first bad decision or telling the first lie, and before you know it, the next bad decision or lie becomes easier. Maybe that is where it began. As a parent, I can tell you that when Jake began his transition from the sweetest boy walking the earth to a combative youth, I had to realize that he hadn't changed overnight. He had been changing on the inside, but for a long time his observable self had fooled us, just as I had fooled my parents and perhaps you fooled yours. I am not placing blame on my parents' predicament at all, please understand this. I was friends with many kids from happy homes who were right by my side engaging in all of the same selfish, devious behavior. We all stole their alcohol and five dollar bills from parents' purses and dresser tops to pay for our pot and beer and cigarettes. We said we were sleeping at each other's houses, but in reality we were at all night parties at homes where other parents foolishly trusted their kids to adhere to the rules of 'no one over while we are gone'. It may be a time of life some of us are destined to go through while striving to show that we were adults, yet our behaviors demonstrated we were anything but. Did you survive these days better than I? How? What are you made of that I was not? This, my friends, feels like a good time to journal, so take a break and think about what you've read. Is any of it familiar?

I have spent much time thinking about where my divergence may have begun. See what you think about this. It may be tied to when I started questioning my faith. I was raised Catholic and indoctrinated to their beliefs through weekly mass, CCD instruction, and my parents' beliefs. I had no choice but to be a Catholic. I got up each Sunday and went with my father and my brothers and sisters; we filed in and headed toward our usual pew. I did this because this is what my family did; it was like being required to do your chores or make your bed each day or do your homework each night. You just did it. But one day you may find yourself questioning why you are blindly following along because you realize you do not believe everything that your religion requires of you. You realize that if you doubt your faith, you must also doubt your parents' values and perhaps even societal norms. In the '60s and '70s, this doubting was hard to avoid as it was quickly becoming a world where almost everything our parents, educators, government, and military told us was not only questionable but was being touted as possibly unethical and corrupt. It became difficult for a young person to know what to believe in, what was real, what was worth fighting for, or what was worth changing for. You didn't want to blindly follow new doctrine though because it may be the same old trap in new clothing. Who can replace your parents and teachers as mentors and role models? I think it was this time of uncertainty where I floundered and at times believed some new, but wrong messages. Again, I blame no one, I am simply aware that I lost sight of who I was, and on my way to discovering who I may be, I gave myself permission to do the wrong thing at times. During such transitions, you have no way of knowing that nothing has to be finite, or that you will adopt many thought processes throughout life as you gain experience through travel and new relationships. You will discard many ideas and also accept many which will become the staples shaping your core values, but you don't know any of this yet. What if you had gone to a trustworthy adult during this time of turmoil, would you have trusted what they told you? How do you even begin the discussion? I know I found myself not liking what I saw in my mirror, yet had no idea how to rectify the situation.

It is interesting because when I look back at photos of myself through this unsettling period, I don't see the joy and peace that had been my persona for a while when the Twiggy and Gloria Steinem influences were fresh and invigorating. These later photos seem to reflect my discomfort and the fact that I was not at ease with myself. I don't look attractive and vital; it's as if my persona was reflecting my inner confusion. Look back at some photos from the time of your life when you may have wandered down the wrong path. What do you see? Continue to look through photos until you see yourself re-emerge into a happier you. It is quite an interesting experience. Watch your body language in the photos; look into your eyes in the pictures. Look at your high school yearbook, reread the notes friends wrote you. How did they perceive you? I am amazed at how revealing doing these few simple things has been for me. I had no idea that I could track my discomfort by looking back through the photos, but there it was as documented proof, now that I knew what to look for.

As I look back on finding my better self again, I realize that I returned to the same dogma which had made my beginning years of high school so much better. I once again began to listen to the voices of change but only the ones that were positive. My deep, almost fierce, belief in a woman's right to choose her path, her right to be considered an equal to men in all respects, and to be offered a limitless future became the foundation I wanted to build on. When you become aware of what your foremothers went through to acquire these rights, you discover you need to honor them with courage and strength, certainly not with deceit and selfishness.

Let me finish up with this. Finding yourself and moving forward isn't ever going to be easy. Yes, some of your mistakes can be chalked up to growing pains, thank heavens. And there will be times where you may discover that you, in fact, do not like yourself. Thankfully, you are not stuck with that version of yourself. You are not confined to being that one person forever and ever. Hang in there, for a new wind will blow in your direction, and with luck and conviction you can move forward to a brighter future of your own making.

On the next pages, think about several things. Think about how you may have moved forward from a difficult time. Who or what helped you move on to a better you? If you did not have a time period as I have described, go back and revisit why you may have avoided all of the pitfalls of your late teens. How were you able to adhere to your moral code? I hope you will go back to those photo albums and yearbooks as I have. What did you see? Tell me.

Entry #5 follows

55

My Thoughts and Reactions

Chapter 5
Defining Moments

I think of defining moments as something close to a 'come to Jesus' meeting with yourself. You know what I mean here, right? I am talking about that reality check whose outcome will impact the rest of your life. Having grasped that something's *gotta give*, it becomes vital that you instigate and execute changes in order to live with yourself. I know, I know, this sounds pretty dramatic, but you will remember that I have previously lapsed into this trait, and I bet I will again. Yet stay with me, for I promise that I will bring this around to something valuable for us to share. If you have immediately understood the significance of what I am saying here, then you have clearly had a defining moment. If you don't understand its significance as of yet, then it's possible you have not struggled with a major internal conflict yet, but I do feel you will eventually. It seems inevitable if you are living a full life that you will face this impetus. In fact, I believe we may experience several defining moments throughout our lifetime, but I credit that first one as the most radical, and it is the one that forever changes life as we know it. It is the one from which we most grow.

If you have a 'defining moment' story, take a moment to reflect on whatever it is now. The intention here is that you go with your first reaction prior to reading mine. I don't think there can be any comparing of our defining moments; we are simply recounting them in order to share with one another as a part of our healing. As for me, I have shared this defining moment with others before you, but only when I see that it will help someone who has hit a particularly rough patch and here is why; I am not proud of this defining moment or what occurred to bring it about. It is still a hard story to tell you all these many years later because I am ashamed of what caused my defining moment, yet I console myself that a sense of shame signifies cognizance, and awareness is the first step to change. Am I suggesting that all defining moments are brought about by regret and shame? I don't know; I don't think so; and maybe you can answer that by sharing some of yours born of positive experiences. I just know that mine thus far have derived from times of confusion and duress.

I shared the episode that changed my life with my son Jake when he was embroiled in the worst mess of his 20 years. I have yet to share it with Josh, but I feel it may be time for that too. After all, if I am willing to tell you, I need to be able to share with Josh. As many of us have experienced, the parent/ child relationship is at best tenuous when your kids are between 14 and 25, and disclosing personal baggage needs to be handled well. Sometimes the circumstances simply arise though, and you plunge in unprepared but willing to risk it. Such was my decision to share my defining moment with Jake because there I was sitting next to him outside a courtroom where a judge was about to decide his fate, and I needed him to know that I had dealt with a similarly devastating situation when I was not much older than he. I hoped that by sharing something this momentous about me, he would see that something good can come out of the worst days of our lives. I wanted him to see who I once was, not the person I was now as a respected, beloved person who seemed to have it all together. I dare say he will never know what it 'cost' me to tell him about it, but in that moment, I understood that it was the best thing I could do for him.

Am I stalling? Maybe a little bit, but let's not put this off any longer; I want to be free of this, and so here is my story. I do need to set the stage, so please be patient.

Looking back I see that I thought I was a leader, but in actuality I was a follower and at times I followed the wrong road. As I have said before in our dialogue, I don't blame anyone but myself because there wasn't a time that I didn't have a choice. No one put a gun to my head, I simply chose to do things that I knew to be wrong because I wanted to. On occasion, I snuck out, or lied about where I was going, drank alcohol, did drugs, and ran with some kids that were dealing those drugs. I know I wasn't malicious; I was simply a headstrong, self-centered teenager focused on her own agenda. These are the facts about me for a certain time in my life, yet I don't think I am that unique. Are you remembering participating in these kinds of behavior? If not, did you know people like me who did? Did you like us or see us as losers? Were you a follower or a leader? Write about it now if you like because journaling may help you see your defining moment differently.

Here is some more information if this is to make sense. I took a year off after high school and clerked in a local grocery store, but I knew this kind of small town life wasn't really what I wanted. I had enough sense to see that I needed schooling of some fashion and I went to college that next year. I wasn't a stellar student, but rather a roller coaster student. One semester I made Dean's List, yet the next I earned mostly C's and D's. I had slipped back into the behavior of high school years without even realizing it. I had a lot of fun, and I also began skipping classes much as I had done before. Fortunately, I did manage to get my Associates Degree in Retail Management and then returned home to work in that field, but I confess I found it lacking. I started out working sales in a nice department store but like most retail jobs, the hours were long and you worked many evenings only to return to an early shift the following day. While your friend's are partying in the local bar, you are standing on aching feet and rearranging clothes racks. I didn't have the patience or maturity yet to understand that this was the process and that I had to earn better positions and work my way up to department manager or clothes buyer through sheer hard work, so I did what I have done before and up and quit. Restless and bored I ended up leaving a decent job and floundered around in my hometown partying and scraping for menial jobs while living a basically useless life. I am sure you recognize the pattern here; of course you do, because maybe it was yours too. If not yours, it was your friend's, cousin's, sister's, or neighbor's because we were out there. I know this to be true because the bars and clubs were full of us. We were smart enough, decent looking, worthy in our own right, but lacking self-esteem because we never really hung in there and earned our own self-respect. Good time girls and guys we were, but don't count on us when the chips are down because we couldn't even help ourselves, never mind you. Time blurs, but one day you look around to see you are hanging out with your younger or older brother's friends or your married sisters. Most of the people who could have helped you move forward are finishing up at their 4-year universities, or have left town for good jobs, or have married college boyfriends with whom you have no history and you feel an outsider. You don't really like yourself or your life and each day is much like the rest. You have enough sense to realize a major change is necessary if you want to save yourself from yourself, but there is one major problem, you find you can't do it alone; you need some support. Sadly, however, you can't even put into words what it is you are looking for. There is a sense of desperation growing in you and this makes you vulnerable.

I found myself in just this state when I happened to see a commercial that seemed the perfect answer to my dilemma. I saw an advertisement promoting joining the military in order to have a wonderful, exciting life and career. There was nothing but opportunity for smart young people like me; join and meet new friends, enjoy an 8–5 job, live off-post in a nice apartment, get money for college, and, of course, see the world. This hit home hard and without any discussion with friends or family, I got in my VW Bug and drove to the recruiter's office and signed up. I was 22 years old, had an AS degree, and I was definitely a 'good catch' for the services who were encouraging female enlistment. The odd thing, and the telling thing, is that I did not investigate all of the services; it was an ad for the Army that caught my attention and that is where I ended up. I naively walked into that office on an impulse, and I walked out having signed a 3-year contract with Uncle Sam. I can only imagine how I appeared to that recruiter that day; he needed no sales pitch, and no work was necessary on his part. Well, maybe one thing needed to be ironed out. The only question I remember asking him was whether I could wear earrings during Basic Training as I had just had my ears double pierced. You see, my friends, I was the original Private Benjamin; yes, I was the woman Goldie Hawn would play so well years later. I laugh now, but wonder how that recruiter kept his face straight. But he did, as a matter of fact; he reassured me it would not be a problem. This turned out to be half true, for you could wear jewelry but not while in uniform during training, and you are in uniform every waking moment. But back to it, I signed the paperwork, got my date of service assigned, and left feeling like the biggest winner on the planet. I had a place to go, a job, a paycheck, a roof over my head, and yes, I knew there would be discipline involved, but I didn't see it as a problem for me. I had been crying out for help in some form, and it was Uncle Sam who came through.

Well, I hated Basic Training as much as the next guy, maybe even more. It's an experience you can't explain to the uninitiated, for only those who endure it know the misery, but it does what it sets out to do. It strips you of *you* and turns you into a part of their machine: a well-oiled machine that can function according to a larger plan. Intellectually, you understand why they do what they do to you; you understand that by breaking you down, they will build you back up into a soldier who reacts to commands without question. They have no trouble using shame and degradation to force you to conform. They threaten, bully, and break you. There is never a moment of compassion or concern for your personal struggle. Eventually, you become numb; you stop resisting their methods, for you just want it to end, and it won't end until you complete every facet of training. The word 'recycle' strikes terror in your heart, for that means you have failed a segment of training and must redo it. The very idea of extending this hell works well as a motivator. You get up, you march, you run, you salute, you scream "Yes, Drill Sargent," you drop and give them 50, you keep your foot locker perfect according to regulation, you scrub floors and shower walls, you qualify with your weapon, you toss grenades, and you endure the gas chamber; whatever they demand, you do. Sound dramatic? Well, it is not, it is truth. You will do anything you abhor rather than stay one more day in that toxic environment. Yes, it turns boys into men and girls into women; it is effective, but it is also the most demeaning experience of your life. While there, I befriended some awesome women and I got through it with their help. We dug as deep as we could and supported each other through each hellish day. I learned what a strong, compassionate person I was in those barracks. My anger at the Drill Sergeants and my desire to prove I was better than they could possibly know drove me to surpass expectations. I would not be beaten down, and I egged my fellow trainees on with words of support when possible. Here is what I did to make myself own my power. We were up each day at 4:30, but I got up a little earlier in order to have time to put on eye make-up. I know that sounds vain and foolish, but it wasn't. I have big blue eyes and when I put on eye make-up, you can't miss them. I spoke volumes to the drill sergeants with those painted blue eyes every day; they knew I hated them. I 'Yes Ma'amed' and did what they said, but I felt my strength grow as I sent the clear message each day. They even started calling me Blue Eyes and that was so satisfying at the time; a victory always renews your spirit. I realize now that they were most likely pleased with my reaction. Maybe they even admired my spirit and gumption; maybe they saw my indomitable will. I know several of my platoon mates did, and I know it helped them take another step forward each day with me. Remember, I went in as a lark for self-centered reasons, but some of these women needed to support children, others were escaping abusive husbands, some chose the service over jail, which was a common practice at one time. Some of my platoon mates needed to make it or return to unacceptable situations. Young, foolish Eileen found herself as cheerleader and coach; a role that was new and rewarding. The truth is we really were a group of misfits, an F-Troop if you will, but by the end of the cycle we won the platoon competition. I swear to you we did! Through sheer will power and against all of the odds we brought that trophy home to those Drill Sergeants we despised, and the look on their faces was priceless. Now THIS, you are thinking, is her defining moment, right? But you are wrong my friends, it comes later and it may confuse you now, but stay with me a little longer.

After Basic and AIT (Advanced Individual Training) I was sent to Fort Lewis in Washington. By now I had settled into military life because after basic it turns out it is simply a job, and yes, I did live off post. I met David and we fell for each other rather quickly. When my unit was being transferred to Fort Hood, Texas, it was a real blow. I made the move, but we somehow became convinced we didn't want to wait out the last year of my service apart from each other. I was in a better position that I had been in before, I was stronger in some ways, but my old personality was never that far below the surface. The old strong-willed "I can do whatever I want" returned. I decided after several failed attempts to job swap back to Washington that I would go AWOL and return to Dave. Yes, I look back on this as my first defining moment and here is why. I found I had one last irresponsible act left in me. I knew I was going to break my contract with the Army, I was going to scare my parents sick as

63

I had to go underground so they wouldn't turn me in, I was going to let down my First Sergeant and Company Commander who had treated me very well, I was leaving my best girlfriend, Jane, to the barrage of questions and pressure she would face as they searched for me. I knew all of this, but I made a bargain with myself just before I left. This was to be the last time; I was going to make myself the best person possible after this, so everyone would not have suffered for nothing. I was not going to waste this chance to become what I now knew I could be; a good person. I felt remorse, and I felt guilt, and I felt fear. You see, I was finally learning the price to be paid for reckless, willful behavior. Up until this moment, this defining moment, I just did things and never looked back or ahead, but here was this bargain with myself. I knew it was wrong, but I promised myself it was the last time and it was. It was still a terrible thing to do, and I did not pretend it wasn't, but for once I wasn't running from something, I was running toward something. Others just saw the rash behavior they were used to; they will never know the cost. They can never know how this final act defined me, but I do. This moment that I chose to do something wrong, but chose so in shame, was what I shared with my son Jake sitting outside that courtroom. I wanted him to see that even with our feet mired in quicksand there is a way forward. I told him so that he might understand this terrible moment in his life could be his defining moment. I told him so he would use it as a lifeline. I told him so he might look into the future of the man he would become. I told him so he would make a bargain with himself; I told him, and it cost me to do it, but isn't that all the proof you need of how my defining moment redefined me?

Now, have you rethought your defining moment? If this gets published as I hope, everyone who ever knew me, or who knows me now will be shocked and amazed at this confession. Or will they? Maybe because we all have a story of a moment that changed us profoundly, it will simply be another small piece of the puzzle that is me, hardly more than a footnote. But I don't forget, and I hope you never forget your first defining moment either.

On the following pages reflect on your important moment(s). Ours will be as different as night and day, but each will be as important as the next. Whatever changes us for the better is worth writing down and worth reflecting on. Thanks for sharing mine, and I look forward to reading yours.

Entry #6 follows

My Thoughts and Reactions

Chapter 6
Looking for Yourself

Do you remember how important it once seemed that we find ourselves? Indeed, it seemed easy when you thought finding yourself was accomplished through things like your choice of cars, music, clothes, hair, religion, or politics. I recall how a person's mistakes and transgressions could be easily explained away as, "Oh, he or she was still trying to find her/himself." As if that was a verifiable excuse for some behaviors. Apparently it did hold some weight in other's perception of you though as you could be forgiven or excused from certain things as long as you were on that self-discovery journey. I even wonder what may happen if and when I do finally find myself only to discover that I am not sure I like what I have found. It also occurs to me that if I haven't found myself yet at 64 then I may never establish who I am, and that my friends may just be the point of this fragment.

Imagine, if you will, leaving this world for your next phase of existence protesting, "Wait, wait I haven't found myself yet!" It is humorous to picture this scenario, but also a bit unnerving too. Do you think that my real issue may be that I don't want to be confined to anything definitive? And another question, do you think it will be discernable when you do find yourself? Will a mirror reveal something that has yet been unseen? Father Thomas Keating, the founding member and spiritual guide of Contemplative Outreach said, "Discernment is a process of letting go of what we are not." His words make me wonder if it would be an easier approach to determine who we are not, because this knowledge may help clarify who we are. As I write this, I am reminded of the scene in Romeo and Juliet where Romeo says to a manic Mercutio, "Peace, peace Mercutio, thou speakest of nothing…" Oh, my friends, am I making too much of this idea of seeking the real me? Do I too speakest of nothing? What about you? Are you a known entity to yourself and the rest of the world? Are there no questions left unanswered about who you might be? Here are some thoughts I have on this subject.

In Chapter 1, I began this narrative with a list of my character traits and qualities, and I asked you to do the same. Yet, for some reason that list doesn't feel the same as this notion of finding myself. Perhaps when I can add the word content to that original list, I will acquiesce to having found out exactly who I am. Paradoxically, I confess that I hope I don't add content to my list because it suggests a lack of yearning for something bigger, something different, something as of yet experienced. Content seems so finite, as if I expect nothing more. The problem as I see it is that I may not really want to be satisfied with myself, or my accomplishments, or my relationships, or my experiences because I wholeheartedly believe I can do better. No, I don't mean better as in better friends, better children, or a better family. I mean that I think I can do better in my existing relationships, and I can keep adding new friends, jobs, experiences, challenges, and ideas. I don't want to become stagnant, nor, I think, do you. When I revealed this thought process to a friend once, she said, "It must be hard to be you sometimes..." I remember thinking that, *Yes, it is hard at times, but it would be harder if I didn't think along these lines of striving for more.* The truth is, I kind of wish everyone thought like me in this regard, and this gets me in trouble because at times I may want more for others than they actually want for themselves. I ask you friends, is this wrong of me?

Imagine if you will that you do accept that you *have* found yourself, and you have to admit that *you* can't dance well, or sing well, you fear heights, you are mediocre at sports, and, oh, yes, you hate running but so badly wish to be a runner. Should you shrug your shoulders while sighing, "Well, this is who I am apparently, and I don't need to work on any of this stuff because one should simply accept him or herself," or on the other hand should you be saying, "I am a pretty good decorator, and I am an excellent planner. I am a physically fit, I am organized, and I love to entertain and make people feel at home. I am a good mother, a good friend, and I am really happy with my life as it is." I guess what I am asking you is would it be better to acquiesce as to what we can't do and celebrate what we do well and simply be at peace? What would be so wrong with this? Let me try to explain why I find this idea of surrendering so difficult. The thing is I wasn't born a good decorator or organizer or planner. I worked at them, I studied them, and I practiced them. I bet if I really did want to become a runner, I could do it, and if I took dance lessons, I bet I could be pretty good at that too. How about you, what is your take on this? Right now spend a few moments listing what you are accomplished at. Now list the things you cannot do well or at all. Take some time to make this list, and then as you read your list, think about what this may have to do with finding yourself or not.

Done? See what you think about this thought. My husband Dave believes that people don't change 'their spots' after a certain age. He thinks after, say your mid-thirties, that you are formed, you are fundamentally the person you are going to be; you have found yourself. Well, I really dislike that idea, and he knows I strongly disagree with that reasoning. It really makes me crazy to think that a person won't be expected to change or improve due to having aged out. I guess I have to admit there is some evidence to support what Dave says. I bet you know some friend or family member who you seriously doubt can ever change. When these folks do things that you aren't happy about, you actually do shrug and think, *Yup, that's so and so; they never change.* But, why shouldn't they with encouragement? It could be as simple as someone being chronically late who now sets their alarm, or it could be as severe as someone who is a chronic liar but is trying to remedy this with professional help, or an alcoholic who now attends AA meetings on a regular basis; what if the people in these scenarios had accepted their traits or faults as unchangeable? Do we write them off, or chalk them up as a lost cause and move on? Therein lies my struggle; this is where it is hard for me to imagine a world where people simply accept their faults, or we accept their faults as such in a world where no one tries or expects a change for the better. What a terrible message this seems to me, and it is one I would not like to be held to. I believe I have evidence that many people think as I do on this matter of not giving up on others but instead hold them accountable in order to help them. Some of these people are psychiatrists, teachers, mentors, coaches, volunteers, therapists, and counselors to name a few. They choose to spend their time offering alternatives and options to those who are seeking change or rehabilitation. They offer hope and possibilities whether it is beating addiction or conquering a fear of heights or fear of public speaking. They send the message that it is possible to change your life with help and encouragement.

I've shared some experiences that indicate I had a very misdirected moral compass when I was younger. I'd like to blame some of the things that I did on youthful indiscretion , but as a teacher I have met so many great kids making the right choices, that I realize it's wrong to blame the teen years for everything I did back then. Choices were made, calculated choices that threw all of my upbringing out the window. What if I had defined myself as a person of low moral character back then and remained on that destructive path? People do, and you know them or of them. We read about them every day and sadly our jails and prisons are full of them. Thieves, murderers, drug dealers, con artists, rapists, abusers, and scammers are all a part of the make-up of our society. But, this is where I don't want to give up or accept that people can't change, that they can't redefine themselves and improve their chances. I know that you recognize the Pollyanna side of me here, yet don't you want to believe as I do? No one should be cursed with a predestined future of failure or held to an expectation that he or she can't improve his or her life and circumstances. I believe that without the continuous positive messages received throughout my life, it would have been easier to succumb to a life without higher ambitions. Although we may not listen in the moment, we do hear those messages… Be a good person, you're worthy, you're better than this, I see your potential, or, you can be a winner. If you want, stop for a moment or two and list the people who were your champions when others were nothing but frustrated with you, and be grateful for them.

OK, I have my list completed and want to share a fragment or two. After a mediocre high school experience I elected to forgo college. I didn't consider taking even one class while working. My parents had separated and were headed for a divorce. There really wasn't anyone pushing me to attend college, and without any focus I was more than willing to drift. My family was simply licking its wounds at that time; we were adrift in the pain, loss, and anger of the recently divorced. Truthfully, there were no words I would have listened to from my father who had left us, nor would I have listened to my mother who was awash in misery. She was in her fifties, still had three out of the eight kids at home to raise, had to face a lifestyle she was not accustomed to, and to top it all off, she had just had a hysterectomy. I said I was staying at home rather than going to school to help her out, and I did help her some, but the reality was that I was being irresponsible and lazy. I was taking advantage of the situation because I had no drive and ambition of my own. I gave myself permission to live directionless under the guise of doing a 'good' thing for my mother. I did get a job in the local grocery store as a checker and then proceeded to party with the other kids who stayed in town. I kept myself in an environment of low expectations, and for a while, I was quite comfortable there. So, where am I going with all of this? I am trying to set the stage for the abject failure I should have become, yet here I am today a worthy person who is trying to get you to agree with me that despite who I had become at that time, it was not who I *was* to be. I had not found myself at all.

Here is some interesting information on this matter of quitting on yourself or someone else. There was a study done to determine something called 'grit' by Angela Lee Duckworth. She was using the grit factor as a predictor of success (Ted Talk, April 2013). Her research seems to agree with my hypothesis that people can change. She found research by Carol Dveck called *Growth Mindset*. This is a belief that the ability to learn is not fixed, that it can change with your effort. When you have the ability to discuss your failures, you are able to accept them as simply stepping-stones to growth (Ted Talk. 2013). I submit that this is not only academic growth, but also personal growth. My ability to use my past bad decisions as 'stepping stones' allows me to forgive myself, and furthermore, to better understand myself. It helps me move forward while doing my best to not repeat what I now recognize as unworthy of me. Am I there yet? No, I am not, I haven't found myself; there are things to be done. The good news about this opportunity to change is that you are moving out of one phase of life and into another, yet you carry these experiences with you on the journey. You are familiar with the behaviors that need changing, therefore; you can identify the signs in others. Because you have forgiven yourself, you can empathize and offer help to others you see struggling to find themselves.

I hope I have made some sense in this chapter because I found it very important to have this conversation with you. I have decided through this discussion with you that finding yourself is a lifelong journey, and that we should never settle for any version of ourselves as finite. Let's return to the vision of me as I leave protesting but let's put a new spin on it, "Wait, wait please…happily, I haven't found myself yet and I need a little more time."

So far, you have listed your accomplishments and weaknesses. You have pondered whether we should give up on people or not. Hopefully, you can think of several people who could use your understanding and support as they try to right their wrongs. People can change, and if you didn't believe it before this chapter, perhaps I have planted the seed of doubt.

Would examples help? Let's finish this up with two important people in my life that I don't want to quit believing can make a change to improve their lives. One is my eldest sister, Maureen, and the other is my husband, Dave. To make it more complex, Maureen maintains that she is completely happy with whom she is, that it is her journey not mine. Dave continues to promise to change; states that he is not happy, and wants things to improve, yet returns to the very behavior that was so destructive to our relationship. Because I can't get inside their heads or totally walk in their shoes, I have only my own faith in the human spirit to hang in there with them. I have tried to quit and walk away from both of them for over 20 years. My sister and I have been estranged for most of those twenty years, yet I still hold out hope for a good reconciliation because I believe one day she will find that she has not found her one true self yet. In those same 20 years, Dave and I have agreed to divorce twice, yet as of now we are still married. I am only here because I do not accept that Dave can't shake off his lethargy and invest in our life. My sister and I struggle as of this writing; we remain estranged due to all of the water under our bridges, but Dave is slowly making a concerted effort. The crux of this is that I just can't quit on them or another human being because I never quit on myself. You decide if I am a fool or if I am onto something here.

Finish up journaling by writing about someone in your life that you will not give up on. Think about all of the reasons that you should simply walk away; now think about why you shouldn't. If you can, go a step further, how will you manage this? There needs to be a bit of strategy here. For my sister, I have occasionally held out an 'olive branch' through an innocuous text. Sometimes she responds, most often she doesn't. I get discouraged, but then as life does, something will arise offering a chance to send out another olive branch, and I do, and then she does too. See how simple it can be? As for Dave, well, we have many things in common that we do enjoy, and I am trying to focus on those. Like most married people, we had dreams for the future, and we have put a few of those things in motion. It is just enough for me to hang on a while longer. Maybe I will decide that I need to leave one day, but it won't be because I quit on Dave; it will be because I will see that quitting on a dysfunctional marriage isn't quitting on the man himself.

Entry #7 follows

My Thoughts and Reactions

Chapter 7
"I Get by with a Little Help from My Friends."

There is little in life I value more than friendship. When we began this conversation, I discussed how fortunate I felt for the friends who have seen me through satisfying times as well as dreadful times, the people with whom I have shared intimate details of my joys and sorrows. Here's to the people who possess the ability to center and heal us when we most need it. With that said, I would now like to add another element to this discussion of friendship, one that requires us to go a bit deeper as we reflect and journal on the very nature of friendship itself. For discussion purposes, I want us to contemplate the idea of three different categories of friendship, for surely you will agree all friendships cannot be equal. I hope you will not only like this way of looking at friendship but also gain some new insights from it. What I am asking of you is to look at your friendships as one of these three categories: as a reason, as a season, or as a lifetime. Looking back at the many different friends I have gained along the way, it appears to me that some friends have come to me at precisely the right season, and, most assuredly, for a certain reason. As a matter of fact, categorizing these relationships has helped me quite a bit when I have struggled to understand why some friendships have endured while others haven't. Read on to see if you think I am on to something.

To get off on the right foot, I want to clarify something with you. When I say friends, I don't mean the many acquaintances we all have. Please don't misunderstand that I don't value this acquaintance role though, because I certainly enjoy these casual relationships very much. It is great to run into them around town, in a grocery store, at a restaurant, or perhaps at the beach or a park. You may pause and smile in recognition and then go on to share a minor event or even sincerely ask about one's health or a family situation when bumping into each other. Perhaps you met these acquaintances at a fundraiser, at a large party, at your kid's schools, or at the gym. When I encounter an acquaintance, I find myself keenly aware of how much I am enjoying the positive, unbiased social interaction. We know enough about each other to have some connection, and we do wish each other well, but we don't seek opportunities to grow the relationship. We are content with this casual status, as we should be.

The nature of the people we call *friends*, however, is very different. My friends are kindred spirits with whom I have developed a deeper bond; our relationship is meaningful and rewarding. My friends are sought after as they are a welcome gift rather than a casual encounter. Interestingly, if we think about it, over our lifetime many of us have fewer real friends than we have acquaintances. Do you find yourself able to agree with me on this so far? Are a host of names and faces flashing through your mind right now that you are assessing the acquaintance versus friend factor, and will you agree with me that we tend to overuse the word *friend*? Maybe we do this because the word acquaintance is too long and formal to use, or perhaps it is because its connotation feels a bit negative for some reason. You don't picture yourself introducing someone like this, "Hi, please meet my acquaintance Mary." An intro like this feels cumbersome and awkward, so we slip into the easy use of the word friend to cover all kinds of relationships. What I want us to celebrate here is authentic friendship and by reflecting on the nature of our relationships, we can do just that. If you haven't yet, list the names of people that you consider true friends. I want you to feel free to go back as far as you need to create this list. I suggest you leave space after each name though, because I propose that you return to the list later and decide if those listed are a reason, a season, or a lifetime. As you read on, I will give you examples that may help you with this process.

I have to admit that I have not been in touch with any high school friends for over 25 years now, yet I can easily name the friends from those years, and I promise you several of them made a significant difference in my life. These friends were the ones who shared those tough teen years; they were the ones with whom I shared many 'firsts'. As I look back on the way we drifted apart so easily though, it occurs to me that these friends were 'season' friends. We came together for a time period in order to survive a time that was all about change and confusion. Because I let these friends drift away, it occurs to me that because I was so restless and ready to leave this season of life, that maybe I had clumped these friendships together with my discontent. It has also occurred to me that due to my lack of moral compass during some of this time, maybe these friends didn't need me in their lives as they went forward either. It is a two-way street, so this is a sobering thought for me. Perhaps I didn't invest enough in those friendships, or maybe I didn't see them as someone valuable enough to maintain a connection. I don't know; I just know I was able to walk away without guilt or remorse. I do not mean to make light of high school friendships, and I have certainly witnessed many of my current friends who still gather with the girls of their youth on an annual basis. I admire this special relationship, and a part of me envies the history these women share. But I also value the fact that they were my 'season' friendships, and as I think of them, I do so with a smile of gratitude. I have surely always wished them joy, happiness, and success. I hope I invoke the same reaction from them when they reflect on our shared past. I hope this helps your understanding as far as 'season' friendships.

When I was in the army enduring Basic Training, I met a woman named Laura. Laura's friendship played a significant role in my ability to succeed in that toxic atmosphere. We connected as we were both cut from the same cloth; we were both hippy girls with liberal ideas who had joined almost as a lark yet certainly as an escape too. We were both 'Private Benjamins' who had expected that nine to five job and living off post in an apartment, and we were both totally unprepared for the reality of Basic Training. We joined forces as a united front as far as winning the war with the Drill Sergeants, and we were successful because we had each other's back. We shared every day of three months of hell and personal growth, but after we left basic, we were never in touch again. I think of Laura as a 'reason' friendship. She came into my life and our union was as real and necessary as any friendship could be, but it was a finite relationship based on our joint need of a friend right then and there; we were each able to leave for the next phase of life stronger and successful without looking back.

Hopefully you understand my stance on season and reason friendships. If you are wondering why I would want to put a label on relationships at all, I hope as I describe my lifetime friends the differentiation will become clearer. What I am trying to get at is that we need all kinds of relationships on our journey; we need the reason and season folks, yet as wonderful and instrumental as they are, it is the 'lifetime' friends we count on most, and we should note the contrast in order to perceive and appreciate their value.

Shall we pause for a moment so you can think about this and perhaps try out this notion of reason, season, and lifetime friends. Maybe this is a good time to reflect on your high school/college years and think about those friends. Are you still in touch? Why or why not? What have these folks added to your life? When I return from my list, I am going to tell you about *my* lifetime friends. Moreover, as I reflect, I am going to be even more grateful for my 'defining moment' because I see the full impact it had on me as a person. My defining moment has enabled me to become a person worthy of being someone's lifetime friend.

So, let's define these lifetime friends. I mentioned that I see these friends as 'kindred spirits' because we share the same energy and intellectual and spiritual connection. Very little, if anything, is off limits in discussion with lifetime friends, and of utmost most importance is the level of trust we place in each other. Lifetime friends understand your actions and even if they don't, they won't judge you. They accept you warts and all as we do them. I can let down my guard with these friends; I can bare my soul. These friends tell me when I am wrong, for they do not fear honesty as they genuinely care about me and my happiness. These friends don't use me for what I can bring to them; their motivation in friendship is purely unadulterated. I make few if any excuses with these friends, for they don't need or expect any. With lifetime friends, the connection is immediate, even if for some reason it is not acted upon right away. Intuitively we sense we are alike in many ways, and we know it when we meet, when our eyes lock onto each other in that first introduction.

Here are some additional thoughts: Even though we are separated by miles, and years may have passed, lifetime friends immediately fall back into their rhythm when reunited. We don't need to be together to be best friends; we are simply better off knowing that we exist in each other's universe. We turn to them when we are our loneliest, and they fill us up. Though we can talk all day, we are just as comfortable in a prolonged silence. When we ask something of them, they answer honestly; if they can, they do, if they can't, they don't, and they tell you why. They won't lose your friendship if they don't drop everything for you as there is no score keeping. Neither of you would ever be selfish enough to expect that. We may articulate our feelings for each other differently, but the bond with lifetime friends transcends words and is understood.

In the preface I told you how fortunate I was to have lifetime friendships. I also told you that I counted on you, my universal friends, and that is the truth. You see, for me, you are my lifetime friends as well. There have been times when I needed you because my other lifetime friends, although they listened and empathized, weren't capable of 'feeling' what I was experiencing. My friend Andrea would suggest turning to a 'closed chat room' when feeling alone, as it helped her through a particularly difficult transition in her life. That simple act of checking in on-line and reading other's struggles and successes gave her the push she needed. I love this idea too, but for some reason it never occurred to me to try this route, due to, I guess, the fact that I am not in the least bit a techy. Or maybe it is because I already had you, my faceless, nameless, but oh so important friends waiting in the wings. I will give you an example of a time that your existence was able to change my outlook on life. My sons, the joys of my life, are adopted and they are the proof of miracles to me. Yet before they entered my life, there were years of infertility, miscarriages, ectopic pregnancies, and let's face it, misery. I have lifetime friends who have shared some infertility issues as well, yet theirs were not quite the same and I hesitated sharing some details of this particular time. When in my 5th month of one of my pregnancies, we discovered that we were having twins. We had only about a week of sharing this amazing news with family and friends before I miscarried at home. It remains the worst time of my life and it took years to move past it. Poor Dave had to handle the mechanics of it alone as he called the ambulance because I had simply shut down after I felt those little bodies, ones I had just watched in awe on the ultrasound, wash out of me. I heard my primal scream of loss resound in my head for many years. I am sharing this worst of times, and I am using the best language I can to put you in the picture, but if you have not gone through this, you can't know. But, here is how you, my universal friends, helped; you see, I knew I was not the first and only woman to endure this terrible event. For a time, I thought I would never recover from this, but because you did, I knew I would. You were out there, you had managed to put this devastating event behind you, and perhaps like me, you kept on trying to have your family. I did not know you to see you, only that you may be walking past me on the street, in a park, or at a business meeting. You had somehow managed recovery, and so then would I. Now do you begin to see your true value? No one else I knew and loved was able to reach me, though they tried their level best, and I too put on a brave front for them. But at night I would lie awake and remember feeling myself lose those little babies over and over again. I knew I needed to stop this, so I turned to you, the ones who knew how I felt, and I told you and you heard me and you healed me. I am so sorry for us that we shared this tragic experience, but I took great comfort in *your* strength, and I found some for myself.

Here's another time I needed someone 'out there' to help me make the correct decision. I was struggling because I found myself seriously attracted to another man; a client. My friends were too close to the situation, and I found I couldn't ask them for advice because it would compromise their relationship within their own families. It felt wrong to include them in this decision as I would have had to ask them to keep this secret from their husbands who were good friends of ours. I mean our kids all played together and we were in and out of each other's houses on a daily basis. This type of situation can arise in the best of friendships, and you have to decide what is fair to others before you burden them. Yes, you may get to unload, but at what cost to them? Do you include them in cuckolding? I felt the unfairness of it outweighed any relief I may have felt in the sharing. But, you know you need sound advice, and that is when your belief in universal bonds helps. This is when I looked to my faceless, nameless friends again, for I knew some of you had grappled with this same desire. I used you as my conscience, and I listened to the advice you would give me if we met. You would have told me that it would come back to haunt me, that wrong decisions for selfish reasons never lead to happiness, and you told me it wasn't worth causing others pain in order to have what may bring joy. You reminded me that as a product of a broken home myself, I would become the one who hurt my kids, and I would always regret this. You told me that any relationship that started in stealth and lies would never be able to breathe freely and flourish. Well, thank goodness, I listened to you. I saw you out there in restaurants, in malls, on trails, and at PTA meetings as we calmly smiled and carried on with our lives. Others may never know what you and I did to do the right thing, but we do. You know who you are, and I know you are out there right now nodding and smiling in recognition.

So, let's finish up thinking about how we 'get by with a little help from our friends' be they reasons, seasons, lifetimes, or, yes, even our acquaintances. We wouldn't be as happy or as sane without them. As the poet Mark Nepo puts it in his bestseller *The Book of Awakening*, "I have been blessed to have deep friends in my time on Earth. They have been an oasis when my life has turned a desert. They have been a cool river to plunge in when my heart has been on fire." Find a gesture to honor friends in the next few days while it is fresh on your mind. Drop a note, a text, or place a phone call. Send a card, go out to lunch, or go on a walk with them. Chat a little longer after yoga or quiz them with genuine interest in the grocery store. One thing I know is that if you are having a bad day, the simple act of reaching out can change everything. An innocent gesture is all that is needed. For instance, just recently a dear friend of mine Linda texted me a simple line... How is your day going? For whatever reason, I don't recall now, I was feeling down on this particular day, but I immediately felt my spirits lift. How had she known it was a rough day? What made her stop and reach out at that moment, for I knew she was away on a trip. Perhaps the same karma that brought her into my life in the first place may have played a role in it; I bet our spiritual connection too played a part, but I resist analyzing it too much as I accept it was simply the *gift* of friendship. I know her reaching out made a difference that day, and our reaching out to others now may do the very same thing for someone else. The power of friendship is priceless, and one it has been pure pleasure taking this time to talk about with you.

If you haven't yet, may I suggest you return to your list of *lifetime* friends, and be sure to bask in the knowledge that you are fortunate enough to have them in your life. I also suggest that you look at your *reason* and *season* friends to appreciate the roles that have played. Assigning categories to these relationships isn't about betraying friends, it is about appreciating them.

Entry #8 follows

My Thoughts and Reactions

Chapter 8
The Nature of Love

Care to join me in talking about something else uplifting? I thought you might, so let's talk about the nature of love for a while. Of course, there are many different types of love, and each one will bring about a different emotional response from you. Yes, it's true that some love even brings about a certain amount of pain, yet I am willing to bet that you would not trade even that particular love for the world. What other emotion makes us feel so alive; what other emotion creates the scars aiding us on our path to change, maturity, and growth?

I suppose the first love of which I was aware was the love I felt as a child for my family. Although my parents were not demonstrative people who daily told us they loved us, what they did very well was to *show* us that we were loved. We had rules to follow, jobs to do, expectations to live up to, and we were rewarded for doing what was expected in a variety of wonderful ways. We had a warm, nice home sheltering us from cold New England winters. We had plenty of good food and adequate clothes and familiar routines. We had wagons to pull and bikes to ride and books to read. We took family vacations, and we celebrated each of our birthdays with a special dinner in our darkened dining room with a candle lit cake. We went to church on Sunday morning, we went on trips to see our relatives, and we watched Disney on Sunday nights at the foot of our parents' bed. For me, this consistency translated into the feeling that I was loved. I was surrounded by a sense of order and discipline which offered security. It was such a basic equation. If X = order and Y = safety and Z = consistency then X+Y+Z = Love. Were you lucky enough to know this formula of love? I hope so, though I am not naïve enough to believe everyone reading can or will agree that this constitutes love. Some of you may have had parents who professed their love aloud every day, and perhaps you were kissed and hugged publically and often. You may wonder at a world where this demonstrative love wasn't part of a happy formula. Others of you may have had to live in an unsafe environment or had financial worries or were subjected to loud arguing. I wonder then how and when you were able to discover that first sense of being loved. Did you have wonderful grandmothers and grandfathers, aunts or uncles, or did some friend's mother show you what love is meant to be? Maybe take a few moments now to write about that first love, that feeling that you were cared for deeply, that feeling that offered you security. Your sense of love may not be anything like mine, but hopefully you can recall who it was that offered you that warm, comforting feeling that translated into being loved.

The next love I vividly remember was known as 'puppy love'. As if that first emotional attraction to another human, aside from your family, was somehow a cute, warm, and fuzzy feeling. Well, I beg to differ because there is really nothing 'puppyish' about the turmoil and uncertainty of opening up your heart for the first time. I had a huge crush on this guy in high school, and I remember that it caused way more angst and pain than the safety and security which I had previously accepted as love. Worse yet, it was unrequited love, though the fact it wasn't reciprocal didn't diminish the extent of the feelings coursing through my body when I rounded a corner in the hall between classes and there he was leaning against the wall in a group of kids. Seriously, my stomach would drop right out and my brain would seize up. Instead of meeting his eyes with a big smile, I would quickly avert my eyes and walk past him as if he wasn't there. Of course, the next step was to berate myself for wasting this opportunity to dazzle him. I mean how was I to win him if I didn't stop playing the foolish game of acting as if he didn't exist? Does any of this sound familiar to any of you? Did you ever go in a tailspin at the sight of someone to which you felt attracted? I know like I know my name is Eileen, that I genuinely wanted this young man to notice me, to like me, maybe even to love me the way that I loved him, but I had no idea how to accomplish this. Face it; I couldn't even make eye contact. This whole sensation was not comforting at all; rather, this love was turmoil, confusion, and disappointment. Looking back as I write this, I am smiling and shaking my head at the foolishness of it all, but I concede it was an extremely important experience to have undergone. I never did win this young man's affection as you may have guessed by now. I know he knew I had a crush on him after a while, but what was he to do with this young girl/woman who got tongue-tied at the sight of him? He had many females who wanted him and didn't ball up as I did, so it didn't really matter to him. The truth is I didn't really know him and it seems I loved him for his looks and popularity rather than his substance; he was just so cute with his green eyes and killer smile. He rode a motorcycle and had a posse of guy friends who wanted to be in his circle, and they fought for his attention just as much as we girls. He was a leader of the pack kind of guy so there was that sense of danger; who doesn't love a dangerous guy? Frankly, I don't even know what we may have had in common to form a real connection; I only know that when I saw him, I wanted him to be mine, and feelings erupted in my gut and loins that I had never felt before. This sensation translated into a new kind of love, and once you have felt like this, you are never quite the same. It was an intoxicating as well as confusing time as you realize that attractions like this are also a form of love, and a powerful force at that. (Note to self: Tell society to rethink calling this puppy love.)

I never did feel like that about any other guy in high school or college for that matter. No one conjured up that same sense of desire and those years were a sort of dry spell for experiencing relationship love. Maybe having survived puppy love, I wasn't quite sure what real love would feel like, and I simply closed myself off to it. Having been raised Catholic, I had a healthy fear of sexual encounters outside marriage and that most certainly played a part for me too. We've talked about boys wanting to 'round those bases' back in the beginning chapters, and fear of the 'homerun' was still very real for me. Yet, during this dry spell from male relationships I discovered other kinds of love. Remember that I have spoken to you earlier about misusing words such as *friend* and *acquaintance*, will you now please hear me out about the difference between the words *like* and *love*? The problem arises because there is a series of things I do where the word 'like' is simply not sufficient enough to express my joy and happiness when engaged in them. While participating in certain activities, the only way I can express my feeling is to use the term love. Furthermore, I need to say that my *love* for these things has not diminished over the years, but rather has grown and flourished. What replaced human love and made me happy and content for several years? Here are a few things I love which could then, and still do, bring sheer joy and happiness.

I totally love being out in nature. It doesn't have to be bright and sunny, for I can be joyful walking in a raincoat with an umbrella through the woods or on the beach. Some of my best day hikes have been under such conditions. Nature is beautiful regardless of the weather. If it's cold, I will bundle up, if it's hot, I strip down, but I need to strike out and walk, hike, bike, ski, or kayak to be perfectly at peace. I enjoy sharing nature with friends, but I can be just as happy alone most of the time. If I am feeling blue or low, a sure fix is to put on some walking shoes and get out to the woods, the mountains, or the beach. I promise you, I feel like a new person when I return. Mother Nature is like a soothing balm; she always calms and refreshes me. When I am enjoying one of these outdoors activities, I feel euphoric as my senses are heightened and a keen awareness of well-being overtakes me. The best part of this love is that I do not have to be perfect in any of my interactions. Truthfully, I am an adequate skier, hiker, biker, and kayaker. I feel no need to excel at any of these activities; I simply want to love doing them, and I do. This love makes no demands; nature isn't counting on me except to respect her and to tread carefully, and that comes naturally. Does nature do the same thing for you? Take a few moments to write about your favorite outdoor activity and why it fills you up. Why, perhaps, you can *love* it.

Another activity, whose love keeps me sane, is music. I know you are agreeing with me here, right? Even if you don't love nature as I do, I know I have you with music. You know the word 'like' is not near strong enough to express how music moves us. It is not an adequate expression for what music is capable of doing for our souls. Can you remember the first song you heard that changed you forever? My song is from the '60s called *Love Is Blue*. I was just a kid, but suddenly I wished I could play an instrument, I wished I could dance gracefully to it, and I wished I could sing the beautiful story of love and pain as told through colors. A simply magical moment occurred when this love of music was awoken.

I had always listened to and enjoyed music, but from then on I understood what music can do to you and for you. Music became a constant companion. I remember my first transistor radio and listening to the DJ and the pop tunes on AM station WPOP. I walked everywhere with that radio, and it changed my world as I listened to great tunes while walking all over town. I sang along soulfully while in the car, and through the years I discovered that many songwriters looked right into my heart and soul and expressed exactly what I was feeling. When I first heard Bruce Springsteen's *Born to Run*, I knew I had found my anthem. To this very day I put on some earplugs and grab my MP3 player full of my favorite tunes and off I go. Music enhances just about everything you do from housework to studying. It is not a distraction but rather a gift. Why don't you stop now and list in your journal some of your favorite tunes. I just did, and I will list them in the back of this book should you have the inclination to check them out.

I **love** to read! No surprise here, right? Books are a dear friend, an escape mechanism, or an academic pursuit. The first book I remember getting was a gift for my birthday called *The Bobbsey Twins at the Seashore*. It was hard bound with a glossy cover of these cute kids at the shore, and it laid claim to my heart. It was mine, and I owned it to read over and over again as many times as I wanted. There were other books in our house of course, but this was special because it was for me. Reading has become much more than a solitary, beloved activity for me; I have belonged to many book clubs and am in two at the moment. Adding discussion to my personal pleasure has been an incredible bonus. I have met many interesting women in my clubs, and I have formed great friendships due to books. I decided to become an English teacher due to the fact that I loved literature and wanted to share that joy with students. I read once where Oprah picks her recommended reads from novels where she is drawn in by the first line. That has happened to me many times, but sometimes, as with friends, you may have to hang in there and let things develop before you see the author's purpose and craft. If you are feeling lonely, pick up a book and immerse yourself in someone else's life. Get carried away to places you have never been, learn about new cultures and societal norms, look up words you don't know and increase your vocabulary. If your family or friends are not available, a book can be a constant companion. A book will serve you well no matter what the reason for picking it up. You see why it isn't possible for me to simply say I like to read, right? For me, it is all about the love while reading.

Before I return to human interaction as love, have I been able to persuade you that there are many forms of love? Do you see how I was able to feel content for many years before I plunged into messy human love again? What do you love that offers you a euphoric high? Is it gardening, sewing, painting, running, or golfing? Think about it and write about it and be grateful for it.

When I met Dave in my early 20s, I hadn't had a serious relationship in a while. Oh, I had dabbled a bit, but no one had laid claim to my heart. But when Dave and I met, I found myself quickly falling for this man who could finish my sentences and seemed to enjoy the same things I did. We liked to camp, drink beer, were both social and fun-loving. I know not very deep right, but we could talk all day long; and we also liked to read the same genres and listen to classic rock music and go to concerts, so he was checking off my other loves one by one. He played on a slow pitch ball team and I happily went to his games and tournaments and made friends with his teammate's girlfriends. We worked hard, played hard, and enjoyed life. We shared the same goals of a prosperous, happy life complete with kids and houses and pets. Eventually it seemed the natural thing to take it to the next step. We had some married friends, and they seemed quite happy moving on in life, and one night on our way back from a party we decided that we would get married. There was no ring, no on his knees romance, no great excitement; we simply decided. Then we went in the house and picked a date in June that wasn't someone's birthday and June 23, 1979 was the winner. I know we were happy, our families seemed happy, and I know we felt we were in love and doing the best thing possible by hitching our wagons together. You know that when you are young and in love, sex is an amazing experience. Your young bodies simply fit together and the pure pleasure of this expression is joyful and overwhelming and addictive. You simply crave each other and having sex every day, and often several times a day, becomes the norm. What a fantastic time of life this is, but if you aren't careful, you may think that this sexual drive is love. You aren't quite prepared for the days that eventually roll around when you are too tired, too stressed, and too emotionally spent to have sex. You may even find yourself worried that you aren't in love anymore when this happens. You have to learn that it is great sex when it is with someone you love, but it also a biological urge and eventually, thanks to biological changes, desire may wax and wane a bit. Yes, this love becomes complicated as life continues to change and kids come along and new jobs are stressful and new interests steal the time to retain that original closeness. Love becomes something you have to work at. We are complex human beings and the reality of all of these distractions is a normal progression. You just keep working at it as long as you can, because most of us want this form of love to remain with us until we die. I remember how much I had wanted to hang onto that feeling of giddiness which has proven impossible to sustain.

Now, I want to share with you my favorite love. It is the love I have for my sons. From the moment I met them, I understood what it meant to love completely and unselfishly, for this love knows no boundaries. Unlike the love you may feel for your partner, who may have trespassed against you enough that you cannot forgive and forget, that is not how you feel about your children. There is nothing I can think of that could dilute this best form of love. Of course, I am not saying you don't get hurt, angry, or even disappointed in them, you do, but that simply does not change the nature of your feelings for them. Two very significant things happened when I first looked into Jacob's eyes. The first was this profound realization that here was someone I would die for. No question, I would do any extreme action to protect him with not a single thought for myself. Right or wrong, I never felt that way about Dave who had enjoyed what I thought was the highest form of love I had to offer. The second profound event was an epiphany, a light went off, and I understood in no uncertain terms how much my mother loved me. She had not been a demonstrative woman as I have already noted. She was calm and self-contained; she was not dramatic nor was she cold; she simply kept her emotions to herself. The moment I looked at Jake and he looked back, that was it. I knew the power of the love she had felt for me. What a gift this was. It warmed me to my soul to have this knowledge revealed as I joined the club of motherhood and what it means. My mother carried nine full term babies, and now I knew she felt the same way about each of us. When I looked into Josh's eyes, I felt the exact same way I had looking into Jake's. I thought to myself, *Oh, welcome beautiful boy, you are the reason.* It's an amazing, insightful moment this comprehension that there is no limit as to how much you will love your kids, no matter how many you have. There are no limitations or restraints in your capacity to love when it comes to your children. You can walk away from your spouse or partner, but your heart cannot walk away from your kids.

I hope you have enjoyed this chapter. I hope you are journaling fools right now. What a great subject to ponder and write about. What great memories I hope have been stirred up. Even the painful moments that love can and will cause are worth reflection. Let's leave with this last thought about the nature of love shall we? Think about how different our lives would be if we didn't embrace at least one of the many kinds of love available.

Entry #9 follows

My Thoughts and Reactions

Chapter 9
Success

How do you measure success? Has how you view it changed throughout the years? I've spent a lot of time thinking about success lately, and I've even come to wonder why I did not write successful as one of my character traits in Chapter 1. Did you put it down as one of yours? I have to wonder, do I not see myself as a successful person? Why not; maybe talking it out with you will help me determine this.

I think when young, we may see success as having attained things of a monetary value. We look at families in large, formal houses who drive luxury cars and wear beautiful clothes on exciting vacations as clearly successful, right? I mean, how are you not a success if you possess all of the accoutrements of a prosperous lifestyle? We assume a man who buys his girlfriend a four or five karat diamond ring is successful; we naturally assume a single woman who can live in an upscale apartment in the city is a success. Success is visible and tangible and as we make these observations we may even feel a bit envious. We may covet this successful lifestyle because there can be no doubt in our minds that successful people must be happy with themselves. I know I accepted this notion of success for a long time, and it's just been recently that I've come to look at success with fresh eyes. How about you friends, what is/was your perception of success? Were you mature enough or astute enough to view success differently than the possession of worldly goods? Maybe take a moment or two or ten and write about your first impression of this topic.

I realize now that my parents were seen as successful, but it's nothing I was keenly aware of as a kid because when it's your world, you have no other point of reference. My father had a good job and drove nice company cars, my family belonged to a

Country Club, we belonged to a private swim club each summer, we went to the beach for 2 weeks, and skied most of our winters away. Because this was my lifestyle, I looked at people who had bigger houses, finer cars, and nicer clothes to see what success looked like. It may seem shallow to me now, but I don't think I can really blame myself for this perception. After all, one of the 10 commandments dictates that we not covet thy neighbor's goods, so it appears to me we were expected to be cognizant of the differences of lifestyles.

Attaining success is a focus for many of us early on. We are taught from the very beginning of our existence to focus on it as a matter of course. Think of it, we learn to crawl, walk, eat with utensils, swim, ski, read, and write, and each time we accomplish one of these tasks, it is deemed as a success. We are rewarded for this success in a variety of ways too. How could success not have a positive connotation when your parents, coaches, teachers, and mentors beam at you each time you master a lesson? Be it clapping, candy, money, toys, hugs, high fives, or simply a nod and a wink, we crave the approval that success brings. We thrive on it. On the other hand, when we do not achieve, we feel the failure weighing heavily upon our shoulders and accept our need to dig deeper, so we can be a success in someone's eyes, and hopefully in our own eyes as well.

When do we begin to crave success? I think it is the first time someone cheers for us. Research shows that we don't actually remember events before a certain age, so all of those 'firsts' deemed as successes may not be part of our conscious memory, but I am pretty sure the collective effect of this cheering helped develop and shape our instinct to succeed. Our ability to evoke such joy in someone simply by accomplishing the task they set before us is heady stuff. It starts out as a very positive experience doesn't it?

My road to attaining success was bumpy at best. In my late 20s and early 30s, I ended up working for Corporate America. I was hired on in the accounting department and then advanced to Customer Service, Inside Sales, and finally to Outside Sales in a large company that sold products to science based customers. This latter job came with a company car and an expense account, and I know I should have felt like I attained success, but the truth is I did not. All I recall feeling was stress because I had no real background or education in the field of science and research, and I felt I was in over my head most days. Sometimes, I felt like a fraud on sales calls and kept waiting for everyone to realize that I didn't know much about the chemicals and reagents I sold, never mind the reasons to choose one pipette or beaker over another. I had never used them. When it came to big ticket items like centrifuges, well, I had no legs to stand on there. Sure, I looked the part in my suits with my briefcase in hand, and I did put on a great front, but that wasn't going to keep me ahead in a competitive field. I drove home to our new bigger house on the golf course each day, yet I knew something had to give because this was too stressful. Mind you, my desire to achieve remained strong, and I was proud of the house and my Chrysler New Yorker; I just needed to either educate myself further in this field or choose a different product line. I recognized that in order to be successful, you need to know your stuff.

In the end I decided that pursuing an education in science wasn't my destiny, so I embarked on a career change by returning to school for something I felt a passion for: Design. I enjoyed my classes and took to Design like a natural. I believed in the value of what I was doing, and I became quite good at it eliminating that disturbing feeling of being a fraud. When asked what I did for a living it was pure pleasure to say I was a decorator, and I admit I did like that very much. Talk about an image of success! Decorator had such a ring to it. I now had an even bigger house, drove a European car, and worked with successful people who wanted their homes to have the right panache. I now felt very good about what I did for my living, and I enjoyed offering what I thought of as a valuable skill to my clients. Things were great, yet I didn't rest on my laurels; I kept learning and working at improving to be worthy of that next level of client, that next hourly rate. As you know, there are many levels of interior designers, and who does whose house in a town is very important. Before I knew it, I was falling into the trap of wanting to do certain houses in town. Was it because those folks were nicer to work with than the wonderful people who I was already helping? No, it was usually the opposite as a matter of fact. I could have remained happy with my lovely clients and remained flattered and pleased that they recommended me to their friends. I had such flexibility at the level I was at; I could volunteer in my kid's schools and have time to enjoy my many wonderful friends. I really had it all and was a total success, but here is what still amazes me, I did not see that then. Meanwhile of course, the bigger house and foreign car cost more and before you know it you have invited your old nemesis stress back into your life as you struggle to balance checkbooks, kids, the ups and downs of business. Dave was in sales and times got tough in his industry, so his bonuses got smaller as expenses climbed. Once again, on the surface we looked like the 'successful couple', but there were fights and worries. Damn, this success thing was not peaceful at all; it was actually beginning to chip away at us.

What about you, do you see any pattern here that you can relate to, or have I lost you? Were you able to simply appreciate what you had? Do you wonder why I couldn't just enjoy what I had accomplished or do you sympathize with my need to keep on striving for more? Have I fallen from your graces? Hang tough, I am going to redeem myself, but it may take a while.

One day, a niggling doubt entered my mind; I started to question whether the world really would end if the perfectly matched wingback chairs and carefully paired loveseats with the artful coffee table separating them hadn't arrived for the holiday party. I had once believed in the presentation of a beautifully and artfully decorated home for an occasion as something sacred. I understood my client's stress level about getting it right for an important event, yet I began to wonder if my perpetuating this notion was commendable or not. Why would I not be explaining to them that their friends loved them, not their perfectly staged home? Was I losing my passion for what I did, or was I maturing and understanding that were more important things in life? Was the contribution my profession offered clientele one that was noble and inspiring or was it reinforcing that possessions trumped people? Unfortunately, I had discovered a void in my work where I had once known only complete satisfaction, and I was at a loss for a while. I did not want to do things mechanically; I wanted the passion to remain, and I wanted the delight I had once felt for my career to return to me. I recognize now that this is when I began to change my views on success, but what to do about it was my conundrum, for I believe that when someone pays you to do a job, you should give it your all. Clients deserve that and for that matter, so do you. If change is inevitable, perhaps you should be listening to your niggling thoughts, for they are your conscience, and as we know if our conscience is clear we are at peace. As the motivational speaker Brian Tracey encourages, "Set peace of mind as your highest goal, and organize your life around it." I knew I wanted peace of mind and I was beginning to understand that the way I was interpreting success was not offering me the peace I was seeking.

Those niggling thoughts eventually lead me to the teaching profession as I have shared with you, but even in my beloved career as a teacher, I was hard pressed to feel like I was a success. Even though I was well liked by my students and respected by my peers and our administration, it was difficult to see myself as a success. I did my job with passion and compassion as I told you from the start, but the teaching field is not an easy place to feel successful because there is always a higher benchmark to be met. Test scores must improve every year and the pathway to these numbers becomes more and more stressful. The system looks at your kids as numbers and scores, but you just want to teach them to love your subject and help them feel some measure of success in their academic and personal growth. You find yourself teaching to tests you are never allowed to preview, which naturally feels completely wrong at every level and this becomes a new level of stress. Sadly, some strong teachers may dread having too many of the lower level classes because they are measured and paid by their kid's test scores. The pressure gets to you, and it sure gets to your precious kids. Instead of celebrating the level 0 kid who is now a level 2, he or she feels deflated because in order to move on, you must achieve a level 3. There may not be a longer, lonelier walk down the hall as the one you make to the office to pick up your test scores knowing some will not have achieved and you will need to tell them so. Morale begins to slip in the hallways, and you maintain you won't let it get to you, but as a human being of course it does. Good teachers leave, and the new teachers need your support because your department must be seen as successful, so you do your best every day, but do you *feel* successful? No my friends, most times you certainly do not.

So, how will we ever be able say that we are successful and, better yet, consider it true? Do you see why I have to change my views on success if I ever want to find peace with the notion? If

I throw away my previous attempts at success where does that leave me? It leaves me redefining the meaning of success from beginning to end. No more tangible accoutrements, no more lofty dreams of wealthy clientele, no more ruled by the numbers, for you see, I have discovered that I am in charge of my own interpretation of success, as you are of yours. I am going to change my attitude about what success means in the last third of my life. I am going to look at being peaceful and personally fulfilled as a goal. I won't worry about what others think of me as much, and I will let go of the notion that it even matters to you if I am successful or not. Chasing the illusive symbols of success, as I used to think of it, hasn't really brought me much happiness, so the heck with it. You decide if I am right or wrong, but with my new attitude, it shouldn't matter to me what you think, right? Maybe reading through this has helped you see my mistakes, and just maybe, it will help you avoid making such mistakes yourselves. That, my friends, I would consider as a success.

Entry #10 follows

My Thoughts and Reactions

Chapter 10
How to Let Go

As evident from previous chapters, I have some baggage. If you have spent time journaling, as I believe you have, you most likely found that you are dealing with some baggage as well. I wonder if you will be able to let go of some of yours, as I am discovering I am able to let go of some of mine *with help*. Shall I give this memoir conversation some credit? Oh, I promise you I do. Because of the help I feel I am getting through writing to you, I have managed to find some peace, and I feel I have dropped at least a 'carryon's' worth. I know, I know, I am sorry; I couldn't resist, for I am my father's daughter, and he is master of the corny pun. But seriously, one should give credit where credit is due. You have helped, my real time friends have helped, and now I am able to say that I am getting some professional help. Some of you may think, "Well, it's about time." And I don't blame you, but in life we are not ready until we're ready.

The poet Danna Faulds wrote in her poem *Allow*, "There is no controlling life. Try corralling a lightning bolt, containing a tornado. Dam a stream and it will create a new channel. Resist, and the tide will sweep you off your feet. Allow, and grace will carry you to higher ground." Beautifully and simply put, and I thank my pal Roberta for understanding me so well that she gave me this poem; she too knows that the first step of allowing can be so damned difficult and seems impossible to do alone. See if you recognize yourself as I talk about the struggle to let go, to 'Allow'.

One of the more grave mistakes I am guilty of is convincing myself that as a strong, hardheaded, Irish girl, I am capable of solving my problems all on my own. Sure, there may well be a collective intake of breath from the many friends who have been gracious and kind while listening to me unburden myself, and you are correct in that you have played a significant role in my sanity. Beloved friends: I thank you, I thank you, and I thank you. But, at the end of the day, even after your wonderful, considered, thoughtful support, I still believed that I alone knew myself best. I heeded your words and advice, but I gave myself the final word. Well, Eileen has been proven wrong in her thinking; I am not a rock nor am I an island, and I need some professional help. Yes, I am finally unloading my burden on someone who doesn't know or love me. She simply has the education and experience to recognize the confusion behind the bravado. She offers alternative views on my truths. I had no idea; I seriously hadn't comprehended that sharing with a neutral person could help immensely and immediately. No, I wasn't expecting this because hardheaded Irish girls are skeptical. Although many of my friends have been able to seek counsel, for some reason I thought I was stronger than them. I believed if I was honest with myself, if I held myself accountable, if I 'poked' my own bears, well, then I would stay ahead of my demons. I was even absurdly proud of the fact that I was my own keeper. I thought of it as a measure of success that people looked at me as a happy, vibrant, sane person who seemingly had it all going for her. Meanwhile, I had this chatter running through my head declaring there had to be a better way to live this one life I have been given. The instigator of this relentless chatter was that Dave and I decided that though we felt we didn't love each other anymore in the manner in which we had begun our marriage, we could carry on through a marriage of convenience. We would share our home, money, duties, and support our kids without expecting anything emotionally or physically in return from one another. Actually, Dave will tell it differently. It was me who offered it up as a solution without perceiving the toll it would take on us as living, breathing, caring humans. Little cracks in the façade immediately began to show though, and before too long we became snappish and sharp around each other. I began staying away from home more because it wasn't an inviting environment and eventually our personal isolation became more than either of us could handle. Dave described his life as one of numbness, for he never knew what he was allowed to say or do, so moments we could have connected on some human level passed unnoticed by one another. For me it was a time of personal pain and stress and that continuous chatter… This is when I knew it was time to get help. Why was I sentencing myself, or Dave for that matter, to such an existence?

Augh, if you want to bail on me now, please do so. This is just a fragment of my life, and you may not be able to relate at all. Perhaps you are so fortunate that you can't relate to any of this. Lord, this may even sound a bit whiny, which is not at all what I intend. You have a few options here: Read on in order to expand your knowledge of a life other than yours. Or, if you find weakness frustrating, well then, write about that and why it frustrates you. In the preface I recommended the memoir *Eat, Pray, Love* by Elizabeth Gilbert. We read it for one of my book clubs, and I remember excitedly anticipating our discussion. I really loved this book and was ready for a terrific discussion with others likeminded. Imagine my surprise when I discovered half of the club thoroughly and emphatically disliked it. Yes, they found the author whiny and self-absorbed. I had loved her honesty; she didn't disguise the fact that she was cracking up and had set out to heal herself. These women certainly didn't agree as did I with the philosophy of the articulate Jungian analyst June Singer, "Just by speaking I can break out of my self-made prison." Gilbert herself writes in her fabulous book *Big Magic* about the controversy surrounding this novel. The reactions she noted ranged from hatred to blind adulation. The mail she received went from "I detest you", to "You have written my Bible". Yes friends, I understand the myriad of reasons you may have to like this topic or detest it. So, if you want to hear me out, read on because if you relate in any way to what I am trying to relay about a time when you need professional advice, you can freely write about it here in this journal, and it may just feel darn good. Finally, if this subject leaves you flat and uninterested, go onto the next chapter about Heroes and Heroines, where you may again pick up the thread, the bond that we have developed thus far. Maybe you can take a moment to journal about seeking professional help in general before you leave us though. Your thoughts on this subject are worth a line or two or fifty.

So, what am I letting go of with the help of my therapist you ask. There are several things I am working on, but of critical importance to me is this notion that I can deal with what is happening in my life alone. Let me say now that my confusion spilled forth freely in my first few sessions, so I must have been more than ready for the release therapy offered. I felt no awkwardness, and I wasn't silently sitting there waiting to be lead down a path. I simply unloaded. I discovered something significant about the inability to mend my broken, unhappy marriage. As you may have suspected, it goes back to something in my past. I shared with you that my parents divorced when I was in my late teens. We kids had watched helplessly as our mother faced her new circumstances, and we watched her struggle to adjust to a life for which she hadn't prepared. As I have previously mentioned, she was in her mid-50s, had three kids still at home, not to mention five not quite so stable older children, and the only jobs available to her were in retail with their low pay and terrible hours. You see, my mother had stayed home and raised her family; she hadn't pursued any career other than homemaker. My father had a good career and made enough money to make this possible, and I am sure my mother enjoyed all that his job and its perks brought to her life. She deserved every bit of it as she held up her end of the bargain very well. After all, that is what a partnership is about, right? You make a plan together, you struggle together, you hang in and sacrifice some together, and then, there it is, the life you dreamed of is actually coming to fruition and you sigh with relief. What she wasn't prepared for was that my father would meet another woman, the love of his life, and he would decide he deserved to be happy with this new love, and he felt he had to leave his wife, home, marriage, and kids. As a young woman, I watched my mother have to sell her house, cut back on expenses and lifestyle, and work weekends and evenings while trying to raise the last of the kids. Yes, she got alimony and an allowance for each child under 18, but it was not going to cover all of her expenses and bills. Remember, my mother didn't want any of this; this is simply what she was dealt. The unfairness of this situation struck me quite hard. I made a mental note that I would never allow a man to leave me in such circumstances. I would always work and have my own money and career so when it did happen, I would be OK. You see, I figured if *my* father could leave us, then someday some man could leave me, but I would be ready for such a day. I also vowed I would not hurt my future family the way my father had hurt ours. I would be strong, always doing the right thing no matter the circumstances; sacrifice if need be, but don't hurt others for your personal gain. I know you hear the young, naïve voice behind these pledges, but at the time it seemed the smartest way to prepare for my future.

So, here I am adult Eileen wondering how I will walk away in order to gain the happiness I believe awaits without doing harm? How can I not? These conflicting, confusing thoughts were holding me back from making some sort of move. I had become paralyzed, yet I finally arrived at the decision that this turmoil was much bigger than me. Younger, hurt Eileen and mature, logical Eileen were certainly at odds with one another. Here is what I learned from sharing this with a professional. First of all, she explained that hurt and harm are two very different ideals. If someone is hurt by my actions it is a residual effect; it is that person's journey to decide how they will deal with that effect of this hurt. It is not for me to tell someone how to handle his or her individual pain from my actions. Deliberately harming someone is a totally different ball game. You cause harm to someone by starting out to do just that; it is intentional, and there is no way I have ever wanted to harm anyone. There is no way my father intended to *harm* his family, for he loved us so; he had to know it would *hurt* us, yet I believe he also had to know that eventually we would accept his choice. We would come to terms with it; we would come to understand his loving another woman didn't diminish his love for us kids, and we would come to understand that sometimes adults fall out of love, even our mothers and fathers. So, what is happening here is that I have learned that I can't keep thinking like a hurt 18-year-old anymore. I made promises to myself, and they were the right promises for me at that time. But as was pointed out to me, I can't keep myself wrapped up in the 'old coat' that fit so well in my youth. I had a right to those feelings then, and my reactions to those events made sense then. But I am not 18 years old anymore, and I am a far cry from the young woman who made those promises to herself. I am struggling because I keep trying to wear that old coat though it clearly doesn't fit me or my life anymore. Here is further proof of that old coat needing to go. If I left you thinking that my mother's life was just misery and bitterness, then I would be doing her a great disservice. My mother became a respected, valued employee who was offered promotions, which she turned down for her own reasons. She was even offered a job as an outside sales rep for Round the Clock Hosiery, but she turned that down too in order to focus on her kids. My mother had a fiercely loyal group of women friends who loved her. My mother traveled all over the world with these friends and sometimes on her own. She was an active member of the Women's Marine Corp WAVES and attended their conferences for many years; she had been a Staff Sergeant during WW11 and was a proud veteran all of her days. She was an avid reader, she loved going to museums, and she loved the theater. She loved nice clothes and she took meticulous care of them. She taught me that owning a few good clothing items was far better than a quantity of cheaper clothes. She had a wonderful life with 8 kids, 10 grandkids, and 3 great grandkids who loved her. Over the course of time, she recovered as humans do from the hurt that sometimes comes our way. My mother did wrap herself in her own coat of pain, anger, and bitterness for a while. It fit her and she deserved that coat. But I clearly see now that when she was ready, my mother shed that coat and began to blossom again. My father and his wife have lived a long and happy life. My stepmother is beloved by all of us kids and our kids. She is warm and sweet and kind and generous and funny, and she loves my father so very much. It is unimaginable to me that these two people wouldn't have lived their lives together; their love has endured and it has been a standard that I was once foolish enough to think was selfish and not necessary. No, I can't let what happened to my parents so long ago color my world any more. It is just an excuse for not moving on or making changes to improve my own relationship.

I am also trying to let go of the fear of the unknown. There is another life out there waiting to be lived. Why should it be something to fear? I imagine it is the uncertainty that is unnerving, although I have done research on rents and divorce laws; I have played with new budgets, and I have tried to imagine myself as a single person starting a new life. And yes, at times I want to stay right here in the convenient place regardless of its problems, and I want to convince myself that it is better to play it safe right here where I know how it works. Sure, it is not perfect, but hey, who gets perfect? I acknowledge that this is a coward's way out; I am not happy and I have spent a lot of time talking about that fact to many people, and now to you. But I don't want to just keep talking and not take action. Yes, you can tread water for a while, but eventually you must strike out and swim to shore. I think going to professional counseling is *me* striking out for shore. There is a strong, vital, exciting woman just waiting to begin her life again. It hurts quite a bit that she doesn't exist for Dave anymore. I know it is my fault as much as it is Dave's, if we must place blame at all. We both quit trying and we surely know the difference; no one knows better than us what it felt like when it was right. It was wonderful, heady stuff. We found all of the answers to life's questions within each other for many years. I can't say the day when I first disappointed him or him me. It was a slow and steady road in one sense, but if I have to assign a reason, I will say that at some point the fundamental outlooks we once shared, well, they shifted and changed for us as individuals, and we never quite got our rhythm back. The art of the deal states that both parties need to make a few concessions, to compromise in order to attain success. A marriage of convenience does offer the benefits of financial stability and security, but when you concede to live together without an emotional or physical bond then you are just fooling yourselves. That is not how passionate, compassionate Pollyanna's live. Dave put it best when he admitted that he was living a numb existence; he was simply marking time each day on a road to nowhere. As soon as he said that, I knew exactly how he felt. How very sad for us both. It was the closest we had been in years, and it was to describe how empty we felt. While you are experiencing this very difficult, trying time, you are keenly aware that you don't want your actions and decisions to hurt your family, kids, or friends. But why would anyone who loves you ever want for you to be living numb like this? They wouldn't, but it takes a professional to help you understand this truth.

Well, I am going to continue to seek help from a professional in this area of my life. There is even discussion of marriage counseling. Dave is also seeking professional help on his own to determine what he wants out of life. Maybe we can figure out how we can go forward honoring and caring about each other's ultimate happiness. When you have cared about each other as much as we have, for as long as we did, what a shame it would be to end with animosity and anger. Maybe if we both continue with professional help, we can turn the tide and rekindle feelings we thought were unsalvageable. Maybe the next session will teach me another valuable truth about myself which may change the entire story and become the next fragment. Maybe...

So, if you hung with me through this fragment, what did you learn or gain from doing so? Is my naiveté endearing or frustrating? Write about me and my belief that I will overcome fear and strike out into the bright future. How about you, have you done this yourself? Write about your success or struggle. I have left out so many of the personal details intentionally because these chapters are just meant to be vignettes. They are fragments that make up a part of my life; it is not meant to be a book on divorce or reconciliation. It is simply an attempt to talk with you, my dear readers, as I continue to make sense of this amazing but at times confounding life.

Entry #11 follows

My Thoughts and Reactions

Chapter 11
Heroes and Heroines

Are you lucky enough to have one or more heroes/heroines in your life? If so, how do these role models impact you on a personal level, and will you take the time to examine the role heroes and heroines play in society with me? I realize that I open each chapter fragment with a series of questions, and I hope this writing style hasn't gotten old for you. My intention is, as the famous Belgian detective Hercule Poirot would say, to get your 'little gray cells' engaged. If we were sitting together, I would be very curious about your life, and I would want to know as much as possible about you, so I think of these questions as icebreakers for us.

Obviously, I have been doing some thinking about the role heroes play in my life. Of course, the role of a hero changes due to growth and maturation, and I think you will agree that we view the characteristics and qualities of heroes differently as we evolve.

As proven through legend, lore, and literature passed down through the centuries, the role of hero has existed since before time was recorded. The tales told by traveling storytellers such as the blind poet Homer, who roamed kingdoms enthralling the town's people with the tales of the epic hero Odysseus, is a perfect example. Odysseus was the wily king who won the Ten Year Trojan War with his ingenious tactic of the Trojan horse. Odysseus and his men had been waging war for almost 10 years, and they were desperate for a victory. He had his men build a massive horse from the wood of their destroyed ships and offered it up to the Trojans as a symbol of defeat. Flattered and honored the Trojans opened the very gates that had kept them safe and allowed this gift to be rolled through to the center of the city for all to see. Unbeknownst to the Trojans, inside of the horse were

115

Odysseus and his men who dropped silently down from the horse's belly while the townspeople rejoiced at their victory in drunken debauchery. Genius! After his victory, he then valiantly fought angry gods, witches, and monsters for another 10 years as he tried to return to his beloved wife Penelope and his son Telemachus in Ithaca. His tale of valor makes him an epic hero, and he became a revered figure. Another such hero is revealed in the tale of the brave Geat, Beowulf, who left his home to sail treacherous seas with his best and bravest men in order to do battle with the evil monster Grendel who was tormenting a beloved king's hall. This tale of fearless self-sacrifice from medieval times is still taught in high schools and colleges as an example of heroism. Yes, these larger than life heroes embody traits deemed worthy of heroism. They were wily, curious, brave, loyal, strong, tenacious, wise, altruistic, and above all, fearless.

Hero legends shift as tales of King Arthur and his golden kingdom Camelot are spread throughout the land. He was a new breed of king who valued all of his knights equally, so he created a round table demonstrating his respect and love for each of them. The legends of this king who lacked greed and avarice introduced a new kind of hero, one who aided those beset by tyranny. These tales speak of a man so fine, so highly regarded it clearly demonstrates society's need for such figures of unparalleled character. I think you can see that we mere mortals needed heroes then, and we need them as role models now as well. Yes, there are countless tales of heroism from every time period and culture, yet there is also the universal truth that no matter the origin of your favorite tale, a person will rise and take matters into his or her hands to serve justice and this act makes them heroic.

When I was a young girl, I recall naming my bicycle Buttermilk in honor of Dale Evans, one of my first heroines. She was the amazing wife of Roy Rogers who I watched on Saturday mornings. Her role on the series seemed as important as Roy's as far as I could tell. She embodied the very same values and seemed just as brave, creative, and dependable in my eyes. I saw her as Roy's equal, and thus for me a heroine was born. I smile as I consider that it didn't occur to me to name my bike after Roy's horse Trigger, for Buttermilk was the steed that proudly bore my heroine Dale.

Showing the diversity of heroines, I recall how I admired the character Pollyanna. Remember I used her as an adjective in my character trait list. In case you didn't understand my reference then, let me clarify. Pollyanna was a character who never lost hope; she found something positive in any situation into which she was thrown. When events threatened to overwhelm her, she turned to the game she invented aptly named the Glad Game whereupon you find a reason to be glad no matter the circumstances. Pollyanna was able to change her whole town with her optimistic outlook, or so the story goes. What young girl wouldn't find her an irresistible heroine? Is she simply a fictional character, sure, but she is based on a societal need for someone to bravely intervene when no one else has been able to do so. Yes, a young girl can be a heroine simply because of her positive outlook.

Oh, there are many female heroines that come to my mind from the indomitable Jo in *Little Women*, to Nancy Drew's sleuthing talents, to Annie Sullivan's success at taming a wild, young Helen Keller in *The Miracle Worker*. Literature offers extraordinary examples of heroic characters inspiring us to try a little harder, and so we find that we do. In a more contemporary setting, I watched with the rest of the world while Ellen DeGeneres bravely came out on national TV despite the contentious media and mood of the country at the time. She is heroic because she very publicly stood up for her right to love the way that was natural to her and so many other members of our society. Despite what must have been some years of hardship, Ellen is now known as the face of kindness demonstrating altruism and tenacity. My all-time favorite hero is Atticus Finch from *To Kill a Mockingbird*. His integrity and sense of justice in defending a black man in a Jim Crow South offered a new version of a hero. He was not a muscular, swaggering, larger than life hero; he was a quiet, dignified, thoughtful man who did what was right because otherwise he could not have lived with himself.

I know I could list many more heroic literary characters and thank many more writers and actors who deliver through their prose and performances, but let's stop to ponder others who prove we have a need for heroes. Where else may we find them? Perhaps you want to take a few moments to journal about heroes and what they mean to you. Again, think about why we need them in society, but also, what is your own personal gain from the heroes in your life?

I would never want to leave out what may seem like the obvious, so I want to mention the everyday heroes that young and old admire. We acknowledge those members of our military services who have fought for our country, and we thank these men and women, as well as their families for the sacrifices they make every day. Yes, we thank the policemen and policewomen, the firefighters, the Red Cross volunteers, the Peace Corp workers, the first responders, the doctors and nurses who rush in without thought of their own peril, and the teachers dedicated to our kids to name a few. Names and faces flash before us because each of us knows and loves one of the aforementioned heroes. But now will you come with me on a personal journey as I offer a few other heroes of mine? I feel sure you will like where we are heading here.

I would like to take this opportunity to say that one of my heroines is the birthmother of my sons. Her name is Kendra, and she is the woman who put the health and welfare of her birth children before her own emotional needs while making the very difficult decision that the best thing for those boys was to give them up for adoption. I have told you that my favorite love is that of loving my sons, and I have told you I am a finer person simply because they are a part of my life. Most of the joy I experience is due to her brave, heroic decision.

Looking at some of the character traits I associate with heroines, you will see why Kendra is one of mine. First and foremost she was wise. She deemed she was too young to care for her child on her own yet, so she made the decision to talk with an agency about what her options were. She went to the Open Adoption Agency where she would be given the best chance of having a say in where her child was placed and with whom. The philosophy at this agency is to protect the birthmother's rights and to ensure open communication between the birthmother and the adoptive family. This may sound easy and logical now, but imagine being 18 years old and being wise enough to walk through that door with only the welfare of your unborn child in your heart.

As are all heroines, she was brave because having made this impossibly hard decision, she stuck to it. As each day, week, and month went by, you know it must have gotten harder to retain her resolve to give up this person in her womb. I know she faced some contradictory reactions from friends who felt she was doing the wrong thing in giving up her baby. She was encouraged by some to live off of the welfare system and keep her child, but she knew that this wasn't what she envisioned for her baby. Her instinct to protect this baby she loved overrode outside interference.

She was altruistic which means a lack of selfishness. Heroines consider the good of others before making decisions. Her unborn baby's future was the most important consideration, and she knew she could not offer him or her stability at that time in her life. How astonishing that at such a young age she was able to put her pain aside and do what was right for her baby.

She was intelligent. She made sure she had an agency that was working for her. She had a certain something in mind for her child, and she went to an agency that would provide her choice. She had a counselor who worked for her, not for us the adoptive parents, and we were aware throughout the process that the agency was working for a birthmother's rights rather than that of the adoptive family's. They were very good to us and we all worked well together, but Dave and I knew if Kendra changed her mind about giving the baby up, the agency would support her decision to do so and help her. Yes, this added quite a bit of stress for us, but you see we understood that this was the fairest way for all parties involved.

She was strong. I have always admired her for her strength of character. Once she committed to us, I knew she would not change her mind. Can you imagine the character it took to keep her promise to allow us to raise her baby? She came to our home and stayed with us before Jake was born, she saw the nursery we had prepared, she got to know us and our philosophy on parenting, and she let me go to a Lamaze class with her. She let me in the delivery room after having Jake, and she let me hold him right away; she let us name him. The next day when she was released from the hospital, no one from her family was able to pick her up, so we decided to drive her home rather than put her in a cab. We drove to her dad's, and then we all went inside so everyone could hold Jake and we could ease some of her pain. When it was time to go, they were all strong enough in that family to let us go with their blessing and love. I just can't say what this meant to me; I still feel the strength in that room as we let our destinies play out. I could never be convinced that this wasn't a heroic act and I know you agree with me.

May I offer one more hero suggestion and we will end this fragment on a high note and set you to writing me back about your personal heroes and heroines.

As a person with a varied background, I feel I have met many different kinds of people. While working for corporate America I met many hardworking people. I looked up to some of those movers and shakers, but they were never heroic in my eyes. In the design field, I worked for many wonderful clients who were generous and community minded. They were inspirational and I admired them but did not find them heroic. It was when I became a teacher that I found some people who I considered heroes and heroines, and though I was privileged to work in one of the finest schools, with the best staff possible, there was a certain faction of our staff that I found then, and still find now as I substitute teach, as true heroes. These are the teachers and paraprofessionals who dedicate their lives to the Special Needs kids. I do not know what ingredient they have been gifted in life, but I do know that our society can't function without them.

I spent my teaching years in the hallowed English hallway. It was then, and still is, a place of lofty ideas and heady discussion. We were a very diverse, passionate group of teachers who believed that what we offered our kids was profoundly necessary. We were creative and dedicated, and we worked long hours far beyond our salaries, because that is what English teachers do. We edit endless papers, create engaging lessons, research new and provocative delivery of the material, we demand the best with the sole purpose of improving our kid's skills, therefore, their opportunities in life. I never doubted what I did was important and valuable, but as passionate as I was, I myself was not a hero, I simply taught students about them.

Now let's move to another hallway to find a different group of teachers. Their numbers are smaller as is their population of students, but make no mistake what happens in those classrooms truly changes the world. Let's revisit the heroic traits again with them in mind. These heroes are altruistic in every sense of the word. The students in their charge depend on them in ways you can't fathom unless you have a special needs child. These teachers and paras are there greeting them as they disembark from the bus to take them under their capable, caring wings. They are wise enough to know that pity for their kids is wasting that child's day, so they treat them with the same respect and expectations any teacher does. These teachers plan full days with measurable activities and challenging lessons, and they hold their kids to a set of standards to enrich their world. Success is expected and encouraged, and then appropriately rewarded. These heroes are tenacious because they have to fight for the attention and services their kids need in a school system where everyone is working to receive a piece of the education pie. They have the patience of saints; they have enough love and goodness in their souls to make sure their charges have the best day possible before they send these kids home to their families nurtured and stronger. They say the measure of a person can be shown by how much they are loved and trusted. The love I see shining forth from the eyes of these students is a testimony I wish for you to witness firsthand. I promise you, it changes you. But these are quiet heroes, and you may find it hard to locate them. Yet if you walk the halls and really listen, you will hear the sounds of singing, laughing, and joyful engagement. You may peak in the door and watch the constant and necessary vigilance of these caring men and women who change the world with love and humor every day for a very special population of our society. I hope I have offered you a glance into the world of Special Ed and the extraordinary people who make this population of students their priority. They deserve our thanks and recognition. Ironically, they do not seek much fanfare, just the support of the community that they and their charges need.

What I hope I have done through this discussion is show you enough to get you thinking about what deeds should be considered heroic. The educators of children in the Special Needs population and the brave birthmothers who sacrifice for their child's welfare are worthy of consideration for their heroic roles in my book. Please think about them and all of the other heroes and heroines I've mentioned, and as you journal about whom you consider to be heroes and heroines in our society, try to think outside the box a bit. I know you will enjoy this subject once you begin looking with an eye toward who *you* consider as the heroes or heroines in your life.

Entry #12 follows

My Thoughts and Reactions

Chapter 12
Choice

Thank God for it, right? One's life would play out quite differently if he or she were not allowed to navigate his or own unique path through choice. If you think about it, our possibilities would be cut in half without choice and so then would our ability to change, to grow, to mature, or to flourish if denied us. I will agree that at times we may contend we have felt forced into a certain course of action, but if you are truly honest, the bottom line is that you did have choice. Perhaps at times you didn't like your options, or none of the options felt acceptable, yet in the end you did find the best one for the circumstances. You've read about some of my choices in previous chapters, and I know you have thought that I made some bad ones, and I agree. That's what we are doing here, talking thru life's choices, but I have many years ahead of me, and I would like to think I've learned enough to avoid repeating bad choices. Now, does that mean somewhere down the line I won't ever make the wrong choice again; I wouldn't want to take that bet, would you? So my friends, do you feel primed for further discussion on this subject? How important is having choice for you, for your family, for your career, or for your spirituality? Take a few moments to jot down some thoughts and flesh them out if you would like. The role that choice plays in our lives is not uncomplicated, and it requires soul searching in order to make the responsible decisions.

Bear with me while I ease into this idea of choice by reflecting on a college class I took in my late 40s. The course was John Milton and the 17th Century. Sounds awful? Oh no, it was anything but thanks to Dr. Dulan. We spent most of the class reading and discussing the epic poem *Paradise Lost* where Milton poses that philosophical question regarding choice through the guise of Eve and the forbidden fruit. God offered

Adam and Eve a life of beauty, grace, peace, abundance, and joy, yes, a Paradise, but he had one demand of his beloved humans. This of course was the infamous edict that they never eat the fruit of an apple tree he placed in Paradise. My classmates and I had lively discussions regarding our doubt that Eve actually had a choice in this matter because an omniscient God knew all the while that she would be seduced by Satan and eat that fruit. Was it fair of God to deny Adam and Eve the apple when he already knew the outcome? Some of us argued that in essence she was set up by God because he was not only omniscient, but omnipotent having the power to stop Satan at any time but chose not to. Others became indignant wondering how he could have set this trap all the while knowing what he would then have to do to his beloved humans as punishment. Some students said it was Eve alone who disobeyed the one rule set before her and Adam because it was she who fell for the serpent's seductive reasoning; as God knew she would. How unfair that Adam had to pay the price; some even wondered why God made Eve knowing what would transpire. Others added if God had interfered by not allowing the serpent anywhere near her, it was then he would have denied her choice. I loved these discussions and found myself swayed at times by both viewpoints. In the end, I believe she bit the infamous apple of her own free will, for she craved the knowledge she was being denied. She must have felt that being told that she could have anything else Paradise offered but this one thing was not an option for her. You can only imagine that Adam tried his best to dissuade her, yet her curiosity-compelled disobedience. Lord knows they faced heavy consequences, but something told Eve that life in 'Paradise' was not worth a life without choice, because in the end, that is what it boiled down to isn't it? Ironically, Adam too had choice in this deed, and he chose Eve.

I hope this wasn't dangerously close to blasphemy for some of you this questioning of God and the result of Adam and Eve's choice. I mean it as an academic exercise and mean no disrespect. It is hard when we enter the realm of religious beliefs, but you see one of the reasons I left my own childhood faith was that I kept running into doctrinal roadblocks. I wasn't allowed to choose how I felt about things such as abortion, birth control, sexuality, or what constituted a mortal sin, so I left in order to pursue my own beliefs along these lines. I would like to be clear about the fact I admire anyone who stands by his or faith, for the foundation of all choice is the belief that if I want to be allowed choice, then I must allow others theirs. Do you agree that this can be a difficult concept at times? We may have to listen to dogma we do not accept, but we should be able to listen with an open mind and hear their reasoning. This doesn't mean we ourselves need to change our minds, and in the end I find good discussion only solidifies my beliefs.

This idea of choice is simple logic, but logical behavior doesn't always allow for our emotional response does it? At what point does this idea of allowing choice become a responsibility? Is it when we approach religious, political, or legal choices? It certainly requires patience, reflection, determination, and understanding on both sides of the coin in these particular circumstances.

There are countless religious sects in the world, and each of them feels that their teachings are the correct path to God. When people enter their particular house of worship, they have every right to find solace and peace in the words of their pastor, priest, rabbi, or minister. The prayers, songs, and rituals are familiar and satisfying and for some the simple act of entering a house of worship can be like a balm to their soul. Many find they are able to go forward with renewed energy and love simply by attending a service. How can this ever be wrong? Well, unfortunately it can because we have to allow that there are extremists who foster a message of hate and prejudice; it is very difficult to admit that these people have the right to perpetuate such negative thoughts and behaviors. Yet, if we want to be allowed our choices, we have to allow for theirs. Happily we can disassociate ourselves from such groups, and we can make sure they act within the law, but as long as they do, we have to allow them their choice. How do you feel about this? Perhaps write in your journal for a while. You certainly do not have to agree with me, and this may be a good time to think about why you do or don't.

How about political choices? Our democracy revolves around a multi-party platform. Anyone can run for office as long as they meet the requirements as to age, residency, and citizenship. I happen to be a registered Democrat, and I would like to be respected for my personal views, and if you are a member of another party, well, you want that same respect. My beloved friends are members of varying parties and religions. Sometimes on beach walks we may touch on the subject of politics or religion, and we hear each other out and our views are welcomed and heard. Due to our friendship, we manage to do this respectfully, and as you can imagine, many interesting conversations ensue. What we do not do is try to dissuade one another from our deeply held beliefs. I feel no threat from the fact we may differ in this area, and I do listen closely to their reasoning while trying to apply some of what they say to my beliefs. I know they are doing the same when I voice my concerns and opinions. I don't think I am acting in a passive manner, and I know some of you might wonder why I wouldn't want to fight or try to sway them to my reasoning, but you see, then I would not be respecting their choice.

How about choices in the matter of the law? You may well ask how there may be any choice when it comes to law, but there are plenty of folks who pick and choose which laws to follow. Some of these choices seem minor like going 5–7 miles over the speed limit. Smoking pot well before anyone talked about legalization was a choice I made. I smoked cigarettes before 16 even though the machine clearly stated what the legal age was. Yes, some laws just seemed 'bendable' to my way of thinking. How about you? Have you always followed every law to the letter? I chose to steal a few times in my youth, and it seemed so innocent, a pack of gum, a candy bar…eventually costume jewelry. Once a group of girlfriends and I went into a local boutique. I think there were five of us and we had pretty much decided that we would each steal a piece of jewelry. This boutique was a small store in a strip mall with limited merchandise as compared to a larger chain store. Can you imagine five girls descending on it at once and immediately fanning out to the various counters and displays? We were pretty obvious. I now know any shop owner worth their salt would have been on high alert the moment we hit the store, but we are talking immature, inexperienced 7th and 8th graders here. Well, one by one we slipped our 'booty' into our jeans or purses and we exited en masse. I remember well what I choose to steal; it was a leather ring which looked pretty cool because it had a small buckle like a belt. Well, we got no more than a few feet outside the front door when we were rounded up by the storeowners. They easily discovered their stolen merchandise and with tears of shame and remorse we gave our mother's names and phone numbers. The storeowners knew all of our mothers naturally, and they were told to come pick us up. No one pressed charges, but it was a scary, eye-opening day for us all.

Choices begin early in life; we had sat around and plotted and planned our thieving; we choose to go steal for a lark. We were all working as babysitters, so we had the money needed to purchase our stolen goods, but somehow we decided that stealing was an adventure we would like to share. Let's look at the other choices here: the shop owners chose to let us go home with our mothers; they knew we would be punished, each and every one of us. They chose to believe we had learned a lesson and wouldn't repeat our actions.

Choices come at us every day, and I maintain that there is nothing more important in a person's development than the opportunity to weigh out consequences and choose. Choose to study, you pass the test; choose to work, you earn a paycheck; choose to eat well and exercise, you stay fit; choose the truth, you have a free conscience; choose a career, you'll be fulfilled; choose children, your heart is full; choose to wake up cheerful, you change your world. You have it; you have the power of choice; you have free will to choose.

Right now I am choosing professional help as I have told you, but I have also chosen to change my approach to life in general. Sometimes we know something is amiss, but because we are creatures of habit, it may take us a while to see that we need to instigate changes. Seeking answers, I started checking into some classes on philosophies I had previously pooh-poohed as not me, not *my* style. At my friend Sandy's suggestion I attended a class on meditation and found the information logical and relevant. I decided to give it a try. I also began attending Crystal Bowl sessions where I learned about Chakras and the affect they have on our life and health. I bought a book of inspirational quotes for each day of the year, for I realized it was far better to think about this positive message first thing in the morning rather than who was murdered or what the politicians were up to. I took all of this information and chose what would fit me best and created a new ritual which has been life altering.

Here are the results of my choices: I set the alarm for an hour I used to think was ungodly, and I rise to stretch and make a cup of green tea. I take the tea up to the bonus room and read my positive thought and reflect on it and enjoy peace and quiet and tea. I savor the words and contemplate how I will use this wisdom today, tomorrow, or down the road. Next, I put on some Zen music and begin a mixed 40-minute routine of yoga and weights, one of my own making which combines favorite poses. By the time this is completed, I am ready for the day no matter what it brings: walks, work, housework, writing, or time with friends. Some of you may be thinking, *Duh Eileen, this is old news; people have been doing this for years*. Here is the best part, I know that, but for some reason I wasn't ready to choose to change my life before. But! Now I am. I choose to get out of my own self-made box and create an atmosphere where I am in charge of my day's destiny. Can you be your own source of change? Will you choose the path to a happier, healthier you if that is what you seek? The essayist Agnes Repplier wrote that it is not easy to find happiness in ourselves, and it is not possible to find it elsewhere. Consider this as you decide if you will choose to make a career change, or choose a new fitness plan, or choose to become a more demonstrative woman, or choose to find a new hobby, or choose to return to school, or choose to plant a garden, or any number of things that you may have thought weren't your style… If you were ready for a change, I hope I have inspired you to choose to pursue it. If you choose the status quo, well, that is your choice too, and be happy with your choice as that is the whole point isn't it?!

Before leaving this fragment, spend time thinking about some choices you have already made, and maybe think about choices you have avoided too. Think about loved ones, friends, and acquaintances you know who are facing some hard choices such as divorce, a forced move, a job loss, or how to handle an illness. How about joyful choices such as gifts, prom dresses, colleges, wedding dates, baby names, career changes, or reentering the dating world? I am sure you will enjoy revisiting your choices, for if you had the final say it most certainly was your choice.

Entry #13 follows

My Thoughts and Reactions

_____
_____
_____
_____
_____
_____
_____
_____
_____
_____
_____
_____
_____
_____
_____
_____
_____
_____
_____
_____
_____
_____
_____
_____
_____

My Thoughts and Reactions

Chapter 13
Never!

Never! I say never again! How many times have you announced this? OK, now how many times have you meant it? Every single time you have proclaimed it? I have lost count of my dramatic never again moments my friends and I wonder if we should rethink this proclamation, for I don't think in the end it has proven to serve us all that well. For the sake of conversation, shall we lump it in with some other words I wish to avoid such as *old, diet*, and *content*? These words evoke a negative connotation for me, and as such, I am trying to avoid using them in my daily discourse as well as my thought processes.

For example, diets usually require a denial of some beloved foods, but if I think of it as making a certain choice simply for a healthier lifestyle, it becomes much more palatable. I now choose a side salad over fries for a lifestyle, not a diet. It doesn't mean I will never again eat fries, especially sweet potato fries, but for the sake of my health, I agree to limitations. But when I do eat those fries, I am going to be sure to find the 'crack fries' my friend Jana talks about at some restaurant in Jacksonville. They apparently are the fries you can't say **never** about and mean it.

The word *old* also conjures up uncomfortable feelings. It makes me think of things that need replacing for they are moldy, outdated, or worn out. When I put a different spin on it though, this is how it could sound, "I am replacing my old hiking boots with new ones," could sound like this: "I am replacing my well-worn, beloved boots because they have given me their all these past few years and need to be retired." Man, I love that. Yes, it takes longer to say it or even think it, but listen to how it expresses so much more. You try; list a few words you would like to replace; I bet you can easily do so.

When I think of a classic never moment, I immediately picture Scarlett O'Hara in *Gone with the Wind* vowing as she raises her fist toward the heavens that as God is her witness, she will never be hungry again! It's a moving moment in the film and worthy of her dramatic proclamation, but be careful as it also foreshadows her selfish, deceitful behavior as the plot develops. Sometimes, when driven to such strong proclamations, one is led to overreact or overcorrect a problem. In Scarlet's case, she suffers not only from hunger, but also from the devastating loss of her pampered, spoiled life as a southern beauty post-Civil war. I admit many of my *Nevers* don't stem from such strong motivations. Mine have ranged from the simple "I will never talk to that person again" to the "I will never eat that much again". How about the infamous never of your late teens to late twenties, "I will never drink that much again!" These words muttered through a sawdust mouth as the beautiful sun tries valiantly to wake you up through drawn blinds while your head pounds and throbs and your stomach revolts. Oh, and then your bleary thoughts wander to the disquieting notion as to what you may have said or done that everyone you know is talking about right now as you suffer through this hangover. Surely you are thinking that is worthy of a *never*, right*? Hmmmm*...

How about the judgmental *Nevers* you've uttered? Have you ever watched another adult handle a situation and thought to yourself, *Well, I would never have handled it that way*. How about watching parents deal with offspring, and you look away disgustedly shaking your head and wondering what on earth they were thinking, so you vow that you will never, ever handle your child that way. Oh, I had such thoughts, and yes they were when I was childless to make it worse; foolish, foolish girl, you know not of what you speak. Yet, the point of proclaiming **never** is a need to feel in charge, in control of your destiny. Each time you proclaim **Never!** it is an affirmation that you can and you will do things differently. Throughout our conversation I have offered up experiences I believed I would never do again. Look at our talk about defining moments for instance. I believed I would never again betray myself as I had when I went AWOL. I made that deal with my devil-self, and it is true, I have not walked out on a contract again, but I have betrayed myself in other ways. Some I will tell you, others I will not as I am not ready, and as we have previously discussed, you are not ready until you are ready. Here is the crux of this discussion: Never is a very long time; it is an eternity. You have no way of knowing what you will face in the coming years or of the choices that you will need to make in the future. You are simply feeling that in this very moment having a conviction to live by is necessary, and repeating *never* makes you feel momentarily vindicated.

How about the "I will never understand why this person has done this" statement? As we have discussed in earlier reflections, you don't know how anyone feels until you have walked a mile in his or her shoes, yet we feel we are able to judge and heaven knows we do. Perhaps the only rational use of 'never' is to state that I will never judge anyone again. I think we could all get behind that, but as I like to think of myself as Shakespeare's sister, I understand that being a normal, human being will prevent me from living up to that proclamation. So, maybe the key is to try to understand why we have done some of the things we profess we will never do again. Consider your first recollection of stating never. Peer pressure usually plays a large role in our *Nevers*. When we were younger, many of us did things we wished we hadn't because we weren't strong enough or mature enough to stand up for ourselves. When I was younger and first dealing with those adolescent boys, the ones who had ideas about what they expected should be happening at parties or on dates, I wasn't able to say no the way I wanted to. I can't fully explain to this day my inability to look some boy in the face and say what was on my mind. Why couldn't I say "I'm sacred, I'm nervous, and I don't feel any urge to do this", or "Please just give me time to figure this out" comes to mind now. But back then I felt I could **never** say such things or I would be ridiculed and talked about in the locker room as frigid. So, unfortunately I let boys do some things I wasn't ready for and then felt shame afterwards. Now, of course, I know locker room talk was going to happen whatever I did, but for some reason, appearing frigid seemed worse than willing, so the guy got to 'cop a feel', as he would have so eloquently put it in that locker room. As the poet, songwriter, and novelist Naomi Shihab Nye so beautifully explained, "I say yes when I mean no, and the wrinkle grows." I recognize now that because I couldn't articulate my feelings, I began distrusting and even disliking boys in general. I began to avoid some social situations where it was expected that people would couple up, and I turned towards female friendships because I felt safer. I now recognize that I turned away from several guys who I could have liked quite a lot, and most importantly, they may have listened to what I should have tried to voice. Maybe they would have even felt the same way. Imagine without that wrinkle...

Here is another, maybe not so profound, but real example of the hindrance of thinking in terms of never. For years I had stated categorically that I would never join a gym. I mean, after all, I can exercise at home, walk for free on the beach, and bike ride while getting fresh air. Gyms were weird, smelly places that people who didn't love nature went. Well, on the path to reuniting as a couple, Dave and I were looking to try something we could do together; something that we would both enjoy. He loves golf, but after 30 years of trying, I can tell you that I do not. I love hiking; he simply does not feel the same way about it. He was already going to a gym and I realized it wouldn't be right to deny us this opportunity simply because I said **Never!** to the gym in the past. I also recognized that if I was going to go, I could be as maniacal about going to the gym as I am about all of my commitments, so this played out well for me as a control freak. A win-win situation. Hey, know thyself. Well, we joined the gym and we started going 2 to 3 times a week, and low and behold I found myself really enjoying, no, let's be truthful here, I found myself loving it. It wasn't just the actual workout part, though I am wicked good on the elliptical and weight machines; it is the people who I love. Every shape and size of humanity walks through those doors. I see women in their 80s using walkers to make their way to the treadmill, husbands and wives who have committed to their health, young couples beginning their lives of fitness together, body builders spotting each other, macho guys, gorgeous women, unmade-up women, styled women, nerdy men with their white socks up to their knees with black Velcro sneakers, handsome guys with svelte fit bodies in their 60s, and overweight sisters championing each other. I see every race, color, and religion walk through the doors with the same focus and desire to change their lives. I don't stare of course; I just smile and as Shakespeare's sister I make up fun little stories about their lives and motivations as I elliptical on a high speed with great classic rock on my headphones. For instance, there is the 'General' wearing his belted chinos and tucked in long-sleeved t-shirt who marches unsmilingly ramrod straight to his machines. There is the woman who wears pastel sweater sets and pearls and yoga pants, there is this older biker dude who wears old fashioned sweats and faded t-shirts with the sleeves cut off, and there is this perfectly groomed tan guy who wears tight tanks and gym shorts and carries his workout book with readers on his nose and logs each thing he does. There is the friendly staff and trainers who always have a smile of welcome as you enter and sign in. Looking around, most of us have on headphones moving to our own beat in between reps or as we tread, elliptical, bike, or stair master. It's all good; no one cares because they are lost in their own reverie. Sometimes I catch a program from the banks of TVs that are playing news or maybe a daytime talk show. I have learned so much watching that show *The Doctors* that I had sworn **never** to watch (yup, you caught me…) I could go on all day because this makes me smile every time I witness this slice of real life. I am endlessly entertained and blown away by the focus and commitment of my gym mates. The fact that I am more fit and have finally reduced my mother's love handles seems secondary. I love their energy and determination. They inspire me. The gym brings my life something that I had foolishly discounted, and it is all the more reason to drop **never** from my vocabulary and thought processes.

Stating never means you can't or won't allow yourself to grow, stretch, and learn more about whom you are and what you are made of. When you put up the **never** roadblock, you cut off the many byways, paths, and trails that lead to the wonderful life you are owed. So, is there a better way to approach never moments? I have thought hard about this, and here is what I am intending. When I am tempted to proclaim *Never again*, I intend to replace it with, "Well, how can I avoid repeating this in the future? What have I learned from this, and why shouldn't I repeat it?" If I am tempted to proclaim *Never!* as I did with the gym, simply because I think I know all there is to know, I am going to state the obvious, "How do you know if you don't try at least once, Eileen?" How about you, care to join me?

So, I wonder where you have gone with your list of *Nevers*, for I don't doubt for a moment you have one started. One of the greatest things about being human is that as creatures of habit many of us tend to repeat the same mistakes. I think we fall into this never trap simply for that reason. Once you break out of old, habitual ways of thinking though, I bet you will agree with me and start trying the things we thought we would never do.

If I have rambled a bit in this chapter, forgive me. I just wanted to follow my thoughts where they led. Perhaps some editor will protest and settle me down. Perhaps I will comb through this chapter myself and think like the English teacher I am and begin correcting as I review. I am not sure what will happen, but I hope I am not too critical of my wandering self so you can see this side of musings too. Regardless pals, I intend to see you on the other side of '*Neverland*'.

Please enjoy your thoughts on the idea of never on the next few pages. You, dear friends, have the luxury of rambling. Go for it.

Entry #14 follows

My Thoughts and Reactions

139

My Thoughts and Reactions

Chapter 14
To What Lengths Would You Go?

Wow, good question, right? But wait, hold on here a moment Eileen, as you've left out the most important part of the question; to what length would you go for **what?** I know, I understand your need for some clarity and direction here, but this lack of direction is intentional on my behalf. I want you to fill in your own blank and follow that thread wherever it leads you. Why? Because though we share such a terrific bond, and there are many areas in which we are able to share, talk, celebrate, and commiserate, it may be that the answer to this question is simply too personal.

Oh, you know me extremely well by now, and you know I am going to share at least one fragment, but I also want to offer you *carte blanche*, or any inclination that moves you because you deserve the freedom to explore this notion in any way you see fit. The best I can do for you is to offer a short list as I did earlier when discussing character traits, and you can use that as a springboard if you so desire. If you have already filled in the blanks, good for you because it is clearly something for which you are ready to formalize your thoughts. If not, here are a few ideas that may help you out. To what length would you go for: love, a job, power, your looks, your family, your friends, money, control, avoidance, self-improvement, improving your relationship, or pursuing your talents? Did that help? I could probably write all day on each of these things, but it has never been my intent to hang around any subject too long lest you think I believe I am an expert on a subject. I am not an authority on anything but my own life. (Well, maybe decorating) You will allow, however, that I do seem to know myself pretty well. What has been a joy, thanks to you, is the freedom to go wherever my inspiration takes me. I do not worry about disappointing you, or, for that matter, worry that you are judging me. Remember, that is not how I feel about our lifetime friendship. I hope I am a curiosity who has gotten you motivated to explore yourselves and that you are having a satisfying experience doing just that.

Recently, I had an experience that has sent me down this *what length* path again. I chose to talk with you about this topic now because I want to prove to myself I am not all talk and no action when it comes to creating my own happiness. So while it is all fresh, I want to discuss it with you for I feel you will get it and understand it. Here are two fragments; one is from the past and the other is so recent the feelings are still fresh. Let's go back first.

Years ago, when Dave and I were separated and planning to divorce, I was looking to reclaim the person I believed I had lost prior to this disheartening time. My very good friend, Peggy, who is one of those rare women totally comfortable in their own skin, offered me a suggestion. When working on her degree she had taken a Woman's Study course, and she recommended that I read one of the books she had studied in the class. I think the book was *Putting Me Before You* and she explained it was a wonderful self-help text and a worthy exercise for many reasons. Well, I'd always admired her sense of self and decided to follow her sage advice. Actually, the text itself proved quite the challenge to locate, but she had inspired me and the dedicated folks at my local library helped me find it at one of the area's college libraries. It was on a limited check out; therefore, I had to commit and get serious. I remember it was summer, and I was on my two-month hiatus as a teacher, and the timing couldn't have been better for me personally. An example, I think, of how the universe will deliver at times. Now, *you* may be thinking I was a crazy girl to spend my summer in deep introspection instead of beach reads, girlfriend time, focusing on my kids, or even lazy days of sleeping in, but I felt a strong need to work on what had gone wrong and contemplate my life's new course. How could I improve my life if I couldn't put my finger on what it was my life was lacking?

What about you my friends, have you ever found yourself searching for answers to the happiness riddle? Will you agree with me that as a society we spend great amounts of time pondering this important question of personal happiness? It appears to me that this question is at the root of so much that is holding many of us hostage, so we best try to get a handle on it. What had started out as a simple suggestion from a friend was about to develop into a life changing experience for me. Because I had now discovered I was prepared to go any length to determine this happiness question, I became excited about delving into this concept of putting me before you, although frankly, it was disconcerting to accept this seemingly selfish notion of thinking of myself first. Ironically, the idea itself seemed the antithesis of some of my core beliefs, but sometimes we need to shake up long held ideas, and this certainly seemed the right time.

As with most undertakings of this intensity, quite a bit of journaling was required while working through the chapters. One of the most powerful queries I was directed to address was the naming of three people that I had loved deeply who had profoundly hurt me. Reading the directive, it was strange how immediately three names flew from my pen to my paper. Without hesitation I wrote down my father, my sister Maureen, and my husband Dave. It was disquieting for I promise you I was not walking around being angry at those three, yet directed to think about it, they appeared like words on a chalkboard before me. After writing their names calmness descended, and I simply absorbed this new information quietly. I think that when too close to a problem, we don't see the obvious, and while journaling and reflecting on these three loved ones, it dawned on me what the connection was. Here is what I discovered with fresh eyes and keener insight thanks to this query.

When you love someone, you may find yourself automatically putting his or her needs and interests before your own. You may even find yourself willing to sacrifice in order that this person feels special. You want this person to know that pleasing them is a priority, and you do it willingly. However, your beloved may not show their feelings for you in the same manner, and this can cause confusion and disappointment. You may ask yourself if this person is doing his or her best to make sure you feel as appreciated as you make them feel. They may love you, but do they put you first? Imagine my surprise when I read that the answer to this question is supposed to be no; they shouldn't be sending you a message that your happiness is more important than their own, just as you shouldn't be sending this message to them. It turns out that you can't be the best person, parent, lover, friend, or partner if you aren't cognizant that your own happiness should come first and that **you alone** are responsible for it. You won't attain all that you are capable of if you don't put yourself first. This concept was vexing as I was talking about my father, sister, and husband, and for some reason their assigned roles seemed to come with a provision that they deserved their station above me. You were taught to honor your father, but honoring him shouldn't mean that you give him the power to control your happiness through the nature of his title. Let me share what I discovered while journaling about my father. I had feared disappointing or hurting him very much, yet I spent years resenting him because I never sat down and calmly, honestly told him how much he hurt my family and me when he left us without telling us the truth as to why. The conversation we should have had never happened because I put his feelings before mine, because I loved him too much. I felt making him talk about something he chose to avoid would have hurt him, so I left it alone and it festered. I could see that I should have talked with him and avoided years of resentment and anger toward him. Is it as clear to you that I caused my own unhappiness in this relationship? Do you see that he was not responsible for *my* putting *his* peace of mind before mine?

In regards to my sister, well, you read earlier how I felt about her. I was so enamored of her and as her younger sister I couldn't fathom myself talking with her as an equal. When she fell off the pedestal I'd erected for her, it was our undoing. I couldn't say the things to her that would have put to right our relationship; I couldn't hurt her because I still put her before me and I felt she wouldn't understand my disappointment in her, so instead I began avoiding her. Ironically, it turns out she was just as fragile and damaged as I in many ways, and she was not any better at life than I. Rather than explaining to her that I had set her up too high and she was bound to fall, I simply let it fester into a wound that we couldn't heal. I put her feelings before mine and because of this we lost years of sister time, too many to count. Actually, we are still estranged, with an occasional olive branch extended. Whatever our differences are, we could have moved past them as soon as I stopped allowing her actions to hurt me. Our unresolved issues are simply a byproduct of my immaturity and I regret that I put her first, because all it did was ruin us.

Lastly, when my feelings for Dave began to change, instead of telling him the truth, which may have given us a better chance of moving forward, I played the same game I had played with my father and sister, and I clammed up. One thing I knew well was that Dave had a fragile ego, as do many men in his age group, and there are simply some things that we don't say to them because it is too hurtful to be honest. So, rather than hurt him I was silent on certain issues and this silence allowed reconciliation to slip further away for both of us. It's so foolishly sad what this withdrawing instead of facing has done to these three relationships. Learning to accept that our happiness stems from our own behaviors, and not others, offers the freedom to live the life we are seeking. As I continue on the hunt for happiness, I know that before I let disappointment and anger at others drive my journey, I will look closer to home; I will look to me first. Deciding that putting me before you will result in leaving the power where it belongs, with me.

So, that my friends is an example of the lengths I will go to in order to improve my one and only life. I will immerse myself, test myself, take the blame when deserved, and now move on wiser. Have you too been able to come up with something that you now recognize as something you have gone to great length to accomplish? What was it for? Again, I wish we were together for this frank, enlightening conversation. I know you have strong feelings about what I have just written and it seems unfair I am unable to hear your story.

I want to share something else with you along these lines. It is something that has happened recently, and it is the catalyst for this fragment.

Because you have more time in retirement, you have more time to reflect on what you want from life, for it can be a time of new possibilities and a time for addressing things undone. The bucket list isn't just a cliché; actually, it turns out it is a weighty agenda requiring serious consideration. Reflecting on this list you become cognizant of the fact that there is a finite amount of time left and you may choose, as Dave and I are doing, to really take stock in order to decide how to spend this final third of your lives. With that in mind, we started looking around for some guidance, something which might offer us new insights for lives that were no longer focused on careers, houses, or raising kids. We also wanted to hedge our bets on being the happiest we could be as individuals with the residual effect of becoming a satisfied couple. With many retirees making up our friendships, we discovered this subject concerned several of our friends too, and through sharing ideas we learned of a program which sounded very positive. We met individually with a representative of a series of workshops and retreats, and we both came away extremely excited about what they seemed to offer. The testimonials presented by the representative were genuine and personal, and I immediately felt drawn to the program. Without much further research, I signed up and paid my deposit. This was huge for me because I am a skeptic, but I was proud of the fact I was taking a step toward progress; a step toward change. In essence, I was doing what my friend Colleen calls "throwing myself out to the universe", and though I didn't have much specific information aside from the sincere conversation I had had with someone I valued and trusted, I felt exhilarated. Part of a path to a fulfilling life, as far as I could see, was abandoning this need to be in control at all times. The very fact that I calmly turned myself over to this program was proof that I was serious about making needed changes. Dave found himself feeling the exact same way and we signed up with no reservations for our respective workshops.

My retreat was first, and I headed off without a single qualm to what I anticipated would be a transformative experience. From the first, I discovered that their philosophy was at odds with my core beliefs, yet I told myself not to judge too hastily because I was in search of new ideas as I attempted to foster change. As the days progressed, I found myself quite distressed and at times unable to participate in some of the exercises and activities. Still, I hung in there in the hopes that I would eventually find some value in their concepts. I did some things I was very uncomfortable doing, all the while trying to convince myself that this was part of the hard work needed for change. By the end of day three, I came to the difficult decision that I needed to leave. I packed my things and said goodbye to my roommates explaining that it had become too uncomfortable for me to stay. This was extremely difficult as I had come to really enjoy many of the women participants. They encouraged me to stick it out, but the fact I so strongly needed to get out of there was an indicator of how agitated I had become, and with little fuss I slipped away.

So, why am I sharing this clearly uncomfortable experience with you now if it was such a dismal failure? It is because I want you to know how far I will go to achieve my goals. I willingly took myself out of my comfort zone, I opened my heart to receive some new ideas, I participated in things I was uncomfortable doing, and I tested myself in order to work on Dave's and my relationship and future. I came home slightly traumatized, seriously I did, and I didn't go out and see people for a few days; I simply hunkered down at home trying to work through what I had just undergone. I found myself sifting through the events to find anything I could use to bring about the change I was seeking. It was through this reflection that it struck me how much I had learned about myself and the best part was that I was able to share all of this with Dave.

Confronting yourself is never an easy task for it would be far easier to place blame on others doorsteps. It would feel cleaner and neater it you could simply assign blame elsewhere and move on. Yes my friends, introspection is not only messy work, it is disruptive to your peace of mind. Yet when push comes to shove, we will be better prepared to deal with life's messes when we know ahead of time what it is *we* are really made up of. If we want others to trust in us, and I think for the most part we do, then we best find out to what length we are willing to go in order to deserve their faith.

Write about a time or two that you have really tested your metal. What were the circumstances, how difficult a task was it for you personally, and did you surprise yourself as to what you were willing to do? I know you have good stories, and I hope you find this a rewarding journal write.

Entry #15 follows

My Thoughts and Reactions

Chapter 15
Commitment

Are you the sort of person who makes up his or her mind and then easily commits, or are you a person who considers several options yet feels no compunction whatsoever to pursue any of them in a timely manner? Are you able to find contentment while drifting from one thing to the next rather than focusing on a specific direction, or perhaps you like the prompt execution of a well thought out plan. Of course, there is no right or wrong answer to any of these questions, so as my friend Ellen says, "No worries." It is simply your preferred lifestyle, and one I am sure that serves you well. Hindsight has shown me that I am a person who commits, which I believe should come as no surprise to you. Admittedly, all of my commitments might not have been worthy causes. Look at my younger years when committing to a stuffed bra, lying about where I was on school nights, or going AWOL for proof of misguided commitments. I confess that it has been through writing this memoir and talking with you that I have become aware of my ability to commit. I am happy that I committed to you, for, after all, we are still here fifteen chapters later aren't we? So tell me, are you too experiencing revelations as you interact with your fragments? I hope so, for our intent has always been about growing personally while enjoying self-discovery. So, what worthy things have I committed to? Here are a few.

First, I am committed to being physically fit, for what started out as an active childhood has developed into a lifelong love of exercise. Admittedly, I can be a bit obsessive in this regard, for I need to exercise; I kind of crave it or I feel restless and out of sorts. I have not been a gym rat per se, as I love doing my own thing, but the gym offers such satisfaction and stability on the hot days or the rainy days when the outdoors isn't the best setting for a workout. Before discovering my love of the gym, I have typically had a piece of equipment in my home, and oh how I loved my NordicTrack. I would get my kids set up with toys or safely ensconced in the Johnny Jump Up in a doorway, and off I'd go indoor-skiing my way to fitness. Later, the kids would play their Gameboys and hang out while I exercised. I believe my boys thought that this is what all normal moms did.

Before the kids, I used to jump rope after work to great music like Marshall Tucker, Shania Twain, and Bruce Springsteen. I admit to being very disappointed when I never got runner's high because what a great way to be fit according to many, but I can walk all day, and that I do with wonderful friends in beautiful settings. As I've aged I have adapted and added a few gentler regimes such as yoga and stretching, but I cannot conceive of a day when I would concede to a life without exercise.

Secondly, I am committed to eating healthy. I am not a zealot, but a believer. My mother cooked basic food and we ate adequate portions. There was always enough, but we did not eat seconds and desserts were offered but regulated. If she made brownies, you got one, same with one slice of cake on Sunday, one pudding on Friday, and two cookies in your lunch box. We were just not encouraged to eat beyond necessary, and I never thought about this much. When I went to college, I put on more than the 'Freshmen 15', more like 20–25. I fell in love with 12-inch grinders, Doritos, and starchy food in the cafeteria. It was easy to spend a dollar on ten-cent beer at the local Ratskeller, and my roommate's parents sent back lots of food when they returned from a weekend at home. I mean great Italian food like cookies, cakes and candy as well as the best meatballs and sauce you can imagine. Yes, my roommates and I ate and drank ourselves happily right out of our jeans and into our boyfriend's! When I arrived home with a rounder face, full thighs, and an expanded derriere, I sure heard about it. My father noted it wasn't an attractive look for me, and my brother Mickey came right out and said I didn't look good as a fat person, his words not mine, but they rattled me. Yikes! I better see myself as they did for a moment. *Hmmmm.*

Weight comes on slowly and easily it seems, and I had never had to worry about it before. Guess I finally joined the world of folks who needed to think about their eating style and make some adjustments. I decided that if I counted fat grams, I could still have beer, wine, and alcohol, so that was the choice for me. Don't laugh; it worked. I knew that I didn't want to lose weight on a diet. I needed to know myself, and what I would and would not give up. By counting fat grams, it led to a very healthy life of vegetables, fruits, lean proteins, and fewer carbohydrates. I dropped down to 125 and was 5'6" tall, so it seems a good routine. I walked everywhere and added some basic exercises. I felt great and have managed to maintain it for 44 years. Sure I fall off the wagon, but as soon as I feel uncomfortable in my jeans, it is back to portion control. I realize I want to be around as long as I am able, and during that time, I want to be fit and not hassled by weight issues. So, yes, committed to healthy eating is a priority. Hey, I even learned how to make homemade low fat Bailey's Irish Cream. A big hit with family and friends!

The best, yet hardest, commitment it turns out is to be the kind of parent your kids need. Sometimes I am not what my kids want, but I promise you, I am always what they need. Now you may be thinking that is just love, but I beg to differ. You can love someone to the moon and back and not do what is best for him or her. I told you about confessing to Jake that I went AWOL and how hard that was for me. But I felt committed to easing some of his fear and to distract him from thinking his predicament was the end of the world. Let me tell you the rest of that story now and how extremely difficult it could be when it came to being the fabulous Jake's parent. I wonder what you will think at this story's end, but well know you will tell me.

Against our better judgment, Dave and I agreed to let Jake drive his friend for a surprise birthday visit to his friend's mother in Wilmington, NC. I could tell there was more to this lovely overture, but he was 18 years old and a part of me said it was time to let him learn how to handle some independence. The other part of me knew that he and this particular friend didn't have enough sense between them, but then how are you supposed to learn if no one ever lets you take those fledgling steps? My own mother had let me go see my sister Pat when she was in college in Boston when I was 16, and I recall that I wasn't totally responsible on those trips, and I sure didn't act the way my mother had raised me, which added to my discomfort and doubts. However that was me and maybe Jake would be fine, or maybe he would not, but it was his opportunity to spread his wings. Anyway, with a bad feeling in the pits of our stomachs, we waved them off for this ill-fated trip.

When the call came, it was to become the toughest test of a committed parent that I had experienced thus far. Jake had been in a hit and run; Jake had done the hitting and running and after a BOLO was sent over the airwaves, he was found. He was also way over the legal limit for alcohol so charged with a DUI, and he was now in the Horry County jail in NC. He had hit a parked car with no one in it, so it could have been worse, but he was in a heap of trouble. The mother of his friend called to give us this news, and she offered to sign him out as the responsible adult if I posted his bail. There was something almost casual about the way she presented this, as if she didn't think any of this was a big deal. In that moment I realized I didn't want Jake to be released to someone who was going to shrug this off, and so I told her thanks, but I believed Jake needed to stay where he was. Maybe he needed time to think about what he had done in a jail cell. I had to work the next day of course, but called the jail to see if I could head down and get him bailed out at a late hour as it was a 4-hour trip down. I spoke to the jail matron to see how Jake was doing, and she said that Jake was still smiling and not acting contrite yet. I asked her if he was her son, would she leave him there another day, and though she did not answer it directly, she said he wasn't scared enough yet. I told her I would leave him there another day, and she reassured me she was watching out for him. I still find it strange how much I trusted her instincts, but I sensed in her job she had seen enough that warranted my heeding her words. Finally, on day number three, I organized a sub and set off to a world I had hoped to never enter, one of bail bondsmen and jails and fear and guilt and shame and lawyers. We had looked up a bond outfit, and I managed to find it, and got my receipt for my son, and then finally found the county jail. When my grungy son in three-day old clothes which smelled of alcohol sweat and body sweat came out, he tried to smile his way out of this, but it just broke my spirit, and I turned and walked away towards the car. He followed and when we got in he said, "I thought you were leaving me there." Well, that broke the emotional dam. I felt awful, but part of me knew that leaving him there had been the best thing we could have done. As hard as it

153

was, there comes a time when that tough love you've always heard about is the only answer if you are committed to your kid's welfare. Jake and I have never really talked about my leaving him in jail those three days, and I would like to know more about the details of his experience, but that is for him to tell me when he is ready. Or, maybe he has just chalked it up as something his mother once did and he has moved on. It stays with me though, yet I never doubt what I did was out of my commitment as a loving, caring parent.

So, what do you think of me right now? Does it seem in character that I would leave my son in jail? Would you have done the same? Have you done the same or something similar that tested you? Write about it now while it is fresh in your mind.

One last commitment story for the road and it's another parenting story, but this one pertains to Josh. Josh is so very different than Jake; really, they are night and day except for their love of gaming. There was less social drama with Josh, but he had his own issues to deal with. Josh is a lovely person, but he has what they call a passive aggressive type personality, and this is compounded by his ADD and OCD diagnosis. His oral motor muscles didn't develop well as a child, and he has a unique speech impediment he deals with too. He was a solitary kid who found video games and computer games way more to his liking than sports or group activities. It was when he joined the band program in middle school that he began to be a part of something interactive, and then when he entered high school, he joined the marching band. Eventually, his guidance counselor suggested he join ROTC, and it turned out to be the perfect place for him. He didn't drink, smoke, do drugs, and he liked the order and discipline. Go figure, I couldn't get him to empty the garbage without a negotiation, but he would do anything 1st Sergeant or Major asked of him in double-time. I am grateful to the Marching Band and the ROTC Air Rifle Team and Marching Teams that he was a part of. These were the only activities he participated in aside from his beloved game systems. In his junior year he decided he wanted to join the Air Force after graduation. We hoped he would attend a two-year Jr. College first, but he felt the Air Force was the career for him, and in the end we agreed with him. He had the full support of his ROTC leaders, and when he early enlisted with a very high ASVAB score, we believed this was going to be the best thing possible for Josh. There was one worry; we didn't see Josh getting as physically prepared for Basic Training as he should have. We tried to talk to him about the focus he would need, and that the more he prepared, the better able he would be to make it through what would undoubtedly be the hardest thing he would ever do. I know it went in one ear and out the other as the blah, blah, blah parents speak to their teens. But when we sent Josh off a month after graduation, he believed he was ready, and he hardly looked back the day we dropped him off. Dave and I sat in the car after the bus pulled away knowing it was now up to him.

Now that we were empty nesters and both sons were neatly stashed in good places, we planned a wonderful road trip and we set off with a full agenda of places we had never before seen. We were on a trail in gorgeous Yosemite when the call came. I was a little ahead of Dave on the trail when I turned to notice Dave was answering his phone. It was a very distraught Josh; he was crying and telling us he couldn't take it. He hated it and he wanted to quit. Man, our hearts went out to him because we knew what he was enduring, and as Basic Training survivors ourselves, we tried our best to pump him up and tell him he could do it. Just hang on kid. In his misery he mentioned that he had also been talking to a friend back home who said there was no shame in quitting, and that regardless he would be his friend and stand by him when he got back home. We quickly told Josh that was not an option and that he needed to disregard this advice. The last thing Josh needed to hear was that kind of talk even though we understood his friend was simply offering him a lifeline to console him. As it happened, we paid Josh's phone bill, so Dave looked up Josh's account and we found this friend's phone number. I called him on the spot and told him to please stop encouraging Josh to quit the Air Force. Yikes, what a crazy woman, right? Can you imagine this poor kid getting a call from me out of the blue and me telling him to back off? You see, when I had hung up with Josh, it was with such a feeling of dread and worry that I needed to be proactive.

Two days later in Lake Tahoe, the next call came. Dave answered it and within moments he handed it off to me as he became too upset himself and he was unable to calm Josh down. When I took the phone, Josh was sobbing; you could feel the snot and tears over the phone line, and he couldn't catch his breath to talk coherently. Here is where I became what was needed, yes, a committed parent. I verbally slapped Josh; I told him if he didn't stop crying and talk clearly so that I could understand him, I would hang up on him. This worked and I ordered him to breathe. It was killing me, yet I kept the kindness and compassion he wanted at bay. He was finally able to speak and he told us that he had been 'recycled', which meant he had to repeat two weeks of Basic Training. You see in Basic you test at intervals, and if you don't pass part of it, you have to join the class coming up behind you and repeat the section you had failed with them. I remember it was something everyone was terrorized of when I was in Basic; believe me, all you wanted to do was to get the hell out of there, and two additional weeks would be an eternity. Add to that you have to join a new group and all of your established relationships are cut off. I tried to imagine how awful he felt, but I knew I couldn't let him feel my sympathy. I just needed to tell him that he could do this; that he couldn't come home and hide in our basement, that everyone had faith he could do this. I said all this in a stern, almost formidable voice. I gave him no room to protest and in the end I hung up telling him that his dad and I would see him at his graduation and that he would be the proudest corpsman there. I was shaken to my core; I really can't tell you how terrible I felt, but I knew it was the only thing that I could have done. I firmly believe it would have been his undoing to allow him to quit on himself. It turned out that Josh was also counseled by a kind female officer, and he later told me the fact that this busy officer took the time to talk with him compassionately had made a huge difference to him. This officer had shown him compassion for reasons I couldn't. The awesome thing is that he did graduate, and Dave and I flew to his graduation and hugged him hard and there we were all three of us balling our eyes out with snot running freely. Reliving this with you, I still feel shaken as I recall his voice begging us to let him quit and come home. He so wanted to be released from what was surely hell to him, but he found no ally in me.

These are tales of two very different young men in two very different scenarios, but each pretty gut-wrenching in its own right. Commitment is not meant to be a cakewalk, for when you commit, it's like taking an oath isn't it?

I hope you have committed to someone or something in your life, and I hope you have stuck with it. Think about a few times you have managed it and what it has meant for you to remain strong in the face of adversity. Maybe think about a time you didn't, and how did that make you feel? I really believe this is an important journal entry, and I think you will all gain from reliving some fragments where you have committed. More than you will know, I wish we were together and sharing these entries my friends, and if need be, we would let the tears and snot flow freely. Of course, that would be followed up with many high fives, hugs, and glasses of wine.

Entry #16 follows

My Thoughts and Reactions

_____

_____

_____

_____

_____

_____

_____

_____

_____

_____

_____

_____

_____

_____

_____

_____

_____

_____

_____

_____

_____

_____

_____

_____

Chapter 16
Truth

Ah truth, truth can be a tricky thing; I am sure you will agree. Would you also agree that there is a major distinction between *telling* the truth and *hearing* the truth? Do you want to hear the truth, and nothing but the truth all of the time? How about telling the truth; do you tell it regardless of the effect it may have on others? I have struggled with truth telling at times, and I can tell you that telling the truth has cost me, and I can also tell you that not telling the truth has also cost me dearly. There is a paradoxical element when considering whether to be honest or not. Should you tell the truth knowing it will hurt someone, or is it better to shield people from the hurt and pain brought about by truth at times? Oliver Wendell Holmes once said that "Truth is the breath of life to human society. It is the food of the immortal spirit. Yet a single word of it may kill a man as suddenly as a drop of prussic acid." His words denote the importance of what truth means to us as a society and as individuals because it reminds us of the power we wield as the imparters of it.

As children most of us were taught that we must always tell the truth, especially to your parents. Because we were raised Catholic, this was an important part of my formative years, and I took it very seriously. If you lied, you broke a commandment and good Catholics were raised understanding that the Ten Commandments were to be obeyed every day of your life in order to gain heaven. As a Catholic, you go to a confessional where you tell the priest your transgressions and asked to be forgiven. Ask any Catholic kid and most will tell you that they lied during confession because they really didn't sin much, yet you had to say something in there as this was the expectation. Most of us were such sweet young kids who rarely sinned, but you had to go to confession to receive Holy Communion, so you tended to tell a little fib or two in order to carry out this solemn ritual. For instance I said things like: "I had mean thoughts about my mother, I was unkind to my brother, or I ate three cookies instead of two." Usually one or more of these sins wasn't true, so you added, "and I told a lie". Sure you did, you just lied to the priest about being unkind to your brother. Regardless, the priest forgave you and you received your penance of a few Hail Marys and a few Our Fathers which rendered you able to receive the sacrament at mass on Sunday. It was stressful as a kid to make up a lie to confess, but I think that is how I began to grasp this notion of truth. A little *white lie* to the priest seemed the appropriate way to handle what seemed to me a tricky situation in that confessional.

Once you've moved beyond the considerations of childhood angst, real life consequences enter the equation and truth becomes even more of a quandary for it involves others. Once you connect telling the truth with becoming a tattletale or a ratfink, you begin to consider the ramifications of truth telling a bit differently. Peer pressure or familial pressure may begin to change your youthful, innocent stance on truth. When your parent asks, "Who broke the vase?" no one wants to speak up as it breeches the bond of siblings versus parents. The time came when I didn't want to see a sibling, friend, or classmate get in trouble because I told the truth, so I said nothing or I claimed that I didn't know. Yes, this is still small potatoes, but it does signal the beginning of choice in truth telling. I would rather tell white lies than betray, and so it begins. How about you, can you remember when you first gave yourself permission to 'fudge' the truth? Try to remember what it was that made you decide to bend the facts.

Maybe we should clarify what constitutes a white lie and when it is allowed. I think of a white lie as an innocent, kinder, gentler untruth. I think it is acceptable while protecting someone's self-esteem or perhaps making his or her day better. I think that the white lie certainly has its place, don't you? I could avoid the obvious such as, "Does the outfit make me look fat?" but if you do care about this person, please tell him or her the truth if it is indeed unflattering. This very subject came up in conversation the other day with my good friend Roberta. She was stating how she counts on friends to tell the truth to questions like that, and that telling a falsehood, and letting her go out in an unflattering outfit would be a betrayal of trust because she was expecting a truthful answer. I hear her, and I second her. Maybe you can suggest that this person unbutton the jacket, or layer the look, or maybe just untuck if you want to soften the truth. Then you aren't simply saying it does make you look bad; you are offering suggestions that could improve the look and resolve the situation. If someone asks if you like their new furniture and you don't, I think the perfect response is, "It is so you!" Because it is them, and that is why it is not a lie, but an affirmation which will make everyone feel better. One more example I want to mention before we move on to bigger issues. If someone asks you over for a drink, and you really aren't up to it, just say so. Say you have had one hell of a day and are beat up and some alone time is just what you need. Friends can totally accept that and feel better because you shared the truth of a rough day. As the demand for truth changes in life do be sure to reconsider your responsibility as a straight shooter, for the delivery of truth is about the most important presentation you may ever make, and you will want to get it right.

I've revealed several times in this memoir when I have been less than truthful. I have come to realize my unease with not being truthful began after my 'defining moment', for it is then that I felt the need to practice truth as a means to becoming a better person, one with integrity. First, I had to stop lying to myself about why I did something selfish or untoward and face the fact that these subterfuges would no longer work if I aspired to a life of morality. Next, I ascertained that the truth usually wins out; it wants to be told; it wants validation, so why add more stress to life by worrying about when and where the truth will out itself? Face your truths head on Eileen and then live with them. It is so simple in theory, but in reality, it is very complicated.

I began to feel truth telling had now become a necessity for me, but what I hadn't considered is that others may not share my new propensity toward it. Should I **force** my newfound conviction of total honesty upon others, because that is what it comes to, doesn't it? In my enthusiasm to live a life of truthfulness, I ended up losing a few relationships because not everyone has the desire to embrace the truth quite as stringently.

Here is the perfect example. I've referenced being estranged from my sister off and on for most of the past 25 years. Once I had decided to live this new life of truth, I decided she should hear what I perceived as her lack of truthfulness with me. I had accepted my lies and forgave myself my trespasses, but I wanted her to know that she, as my older sister, should have offered me sage advice back then; she should have been a role model in my life and she should have shown me the right path. This is where I believed my truth had led me. I thought she owed me an answer as to why she didn't do any of those things because surely she could have stopped me from making many of those mistakes, and I wanted her to tell me the truth about why she hadn't. By now, you all see that what I was doing here was trying to place my lack of character on her; Eileen was on a crusade for truth but blind to her own blame. 'My truth' was actually an assault on her character, and she rightfully took it that way. Her only choice was to be defensive, which you can appreciate was the correct and natural reaction. Now, you would think that I would have learned from this failed attempt at forcing truth, but it appears I did not. Throughout the years, I periodically kept at her demanding she be the older sister she should be, and our new, better relationship could begin as soon as she told me her truths. I felt very strongly that she was struggling at times because she wouldn't face certain truths; good heavens it was like I wanted to be hear her confession or something. It's painful for me as I now see how overbearing I must have been in my relentless pursuit to save her from herself. How full of myself I must have seemed to her. As you well know, my insistence drove her away, as well it should. My god, I hope I am not driving you away my dear readers. You see, I used to question without truth what good was any relationship? To my way of thinking it was a fake relationship and therefore not worth having. I even went so far as to think it insulted my intelligence when others weren't truthful with me. Imagine if my younger sister had approached me and demanded the truth as to why I was less than a great sister to her, I would like to think I would have said, "Yes, Nancy, I am so sorry, but I was immature and insecure and trying to be cool and not even thinking about you whatsoever." My truthful answer would of course solve all Nancy's problems and change her past right? NO, it would not, but it might make her feel better, which may be what I was seeking. I have come to realize that my older sister had her own worries, ones I could not even fathom as I was five years younger, and the truth of the matter is that she was not put on this earth to be my conscience or keeper. My lesson here is that living your life of truth is your choice, and it needs to be done carefully and correctly. Please don't put your newfound standards on others shoulders. Having a relationship with someone does not have to rely solely on truth. As my sister Pat explains, there are many ways to connect on many different levels. She simply keeps to banal conversations and plays board games and asks innocuous questions that don't demand deep responses. If that is what the other person needs or wants, who are we to deny them? So, let's learn from my sister and lighten up before we lose the very relationship we were attempting to regain.

Did that anecdote of my botched attempt at truth-forcing transport you to a time in your life when forcing the truth backfired on you? Maybe you handled it better and capably delivered the truth well enough to recover something important in your life. Spend some time journaling about a time telling the truth worked or didn't work for you. You will see it more clearly through hindsight.

So now, let's talk about when I opted *not* to tell the truth and how that backfired on me as well. Don't get me wrong, my experiences with truth are not all bad, but for many reasons these fragments feel like the right ones to share. Maybe others of you out there have dealt with these same problems of truth, and need to know you are not alone in a struggle to balance a truthful lifestyle and still maintain peace within relationships. As we have stated, truth can be a tricky business.

When Dave and I began the long, slow process of drifting apart, there were many missed opportunities on both of our parts. Looking back, it was my pigheadedness that was my worst enemy. Remember way back to the beginning traits where I told you that I have a tendency to cut off my nose to spite my face; see if you witness it here. Instead of being honest enough to share with Dave that his lethargic temperament was slowly and steadily killing the love I felt for him, I stayed silent and waited for him to ask me what was wrong. I vividly remember feeling that if I had to *tell* him what to do to make me/us happy, then it wasn't genuine. He should know what I was looking for from him in our relationship. I mean, we had been married a long time, and I felt he should know me better than anyone. If I had to *tell* him what to say and do, what was the point? I promise you, I honestly felt this way. It didn't make me happy, but I know I profoundly believed that he should make a move to save us, and if he didn't, then I wasn't going to be the one to do that on top of everything else I felt I was doing. Sounds so foolish now, and I wonder what it was I thought I was doing that was more important that helping us? Maybe it was working, mothering, housekeeping, cleaning, helping with the yard…yet it was so counterintuitive of me, and I now see that I set him up to fail by not simply talking honestly with him about my feelings. I had witnessed other men we knew taking steps to find out how to resolve marital difficulties, therefore, I believed he should be doing it too. In other words, I thought he was choosing to do nothing intentionally out of sheer laziness or apathy. The more he sat in his chair reading the paper and watching sports and not participating with the boys and me, the angrier I got. Yes, it seems it was easier to become angry but not truthful. By not communicating the truth, I was enabling Dave's behavior, well actually his lack thereof. I chalked up disappointment after disappointment like points on a scoreboard, one he had no idea I was keeping. I simply allowed him to hang himself.

Oh, what a waste of your lives together you must be thinking right now; why didn't she just speak up and take action, and you are right to question me, for the farther apart we became, the harder the road back would become. That is what happens when you are pigheaded and withhold the truth my friends. Because truth delivered well and respectfully should open doors leading to a better understanding of one another. Eventually I did speak up and tell Dave, but it didn't come out well as it was delivered in an angry accusatory tone, and by then it just caused a bigger breach.

As the Irish poet and playwright Oscar Wilde once said, "The truth is rarely pure and never simple," such a succinct and elegant way to cover such a weighty topic. I hope you can agree that we don't have the right to turn someone else's life upside down by withholding the truth or, conversely, by forcing it upon those who do not wish to partake of it. You've heard the saying,

"The truth will set you free," and I wouldn't disagree with that, but it is how you present the material that makes all the difference.

So, what is your reaction to this discussion of truth? Have these musing made you rethink how important truth is? At the very least, I hope you were able to stop and ponder what *your* truth is. How has dealing in truth affected your life and relationships? Maybe write about how you can best use truth to bring about a change to your life. Whatever you put down in this journal, it is going to help you gain some clarity on how to handle situations a little differently. You can see it has categorically helped me. As always, thanks for your time and attention and friendship.

Entry #17 follows

My Thoughts and Reactions

Chapter 17
Beliefs

Most of us have something in which we deeply believe. For some of us, these beliefs are the foundation of what make us loving, caring human beings. We find ourselves basing many of our decisions on our belief system because of the faith we place in it. Our beliefs become the fundamental basis, the cornerstone if you will, for the majority of our actions. How is it then that such an intricate component of our society can be based on something that is so personal, varied, and diverse? How do we hold true to our own belief system, yet allow for another person's perspective when it may be in opposition to ours? It's a big question, and one most of us deal with on a daily basis living as we do in a democracy.

The Human Truth Foundation, an organization committed to inspiring deep thought on beliefs, currently lists 81 entries for Belief Systems, but they also state that it is simply impossible to list all varieties of religion as we as a species have created an almost infinite variety of religious and transcendental ideas. I agree that the sheer variety of beliefs can be overwhelming and it would require a lifetime of study, not to mention that most of us have neither the time nor the inclination to pursue this on an academic level. However historians and theologians are so inclined and due to their research it is safe to say we know that throughout history there is ample evidence that believing in *something* or *someone* is a critical component of the human race's survival. Many of us feel the natural pull toward a doctrine which offers peace, solace, and reason. And like many of those who came before, our belief system begins when we are children as it is introduced to us by our parents. We love and trust our parents, so we happily learn our prayers, read the gospels and psalms, obey the commandments, and count off on our rosary beads. It is a comfortable and familiar feeling when you gaze around your place of worship knowing you are a part of something mysterious and solemn and beautiful. I remember just such rewards. I remember as a young child feeling I should become a nun and turn myself over to prayer and servitude. It seemed so noble. Knowing me as I do now, I bet it was actually because of TV shows such as *The Flying Nun* with the adorable Sally Field, or the movie where the irrepressible novitiate Maria sang her way into our hearts in *The Sound of Music*, or the movie where Mary Tyler Moore and Elvis Presley find each other in the inner city in *Change of Habit*. These movies and shows were impossibly romantic to a young, impressionable girl, and I could easily see myself in any of those roles for a while. But as you mature and become a part of the dialogue, not just the vessel for others ideas and beliefs, you become aware that beliefs are not based on TV shows, musicals, or melodramatic movies, not even necessarily based on your parents' beliefs. It can become quite challenging and confusing when you begin to question long held beliefs while incorporating some new, personal thoughts on ideology. It becomes a complex road to travel as you seek a system that sustains and comforts you not only here on this earth, but also one which offers a life *ever after*.

I wonder if you would like to stop here and journal your authentic and immediate reaction as to what your belief system is. Record how it makes you feel and the role it plays in your daily life. Does your belief system offer comfort and peace or are you still seeking one to this very day? Maybe you have never struggled because your system has always offered you inner peace. If so, write about that and be grateful for its comfort.

Thinking about beliefs should be uplifting and reassuring. Here is where my journal journey took me on this subject. I have this very special niece Courtney (actually, all my nieces and nephews are pretty great, but Courtney and I have a wonderful bond). Courtney is very bright, quirky, talented, creative, and a bit OCD, which is something I understand because my son Josh is OCD as well. She and I loved to take long walks whenever our families got together, and we talked about everything under the sun. On one particularly long walk, she broached the subject of what I believed on a spiritual level. Courtney strongly embraced the existence of ghosts as a part of her belief system; for her they

170

weren't scary, worrisome creatures of terror, they were just spirits who needed some help on their journey. Truthfully, I couldn't refute her thought process, nor did I try as I have my own belief system which can't be proven either. Her mother knew of her beliefs, so I didn't feel I was supposed to reassure her that there was no such thing as ghosts but rather to hear her out as we walked, and then I shared what I held to be true. I did want to tread lightly as I responded, but I also wanted to be honest in this very academic conversation. Here is what I told my 16-year-old niece.

I don't believe in an angry, vengeful god, and I don't believe in heaven or hell, but rather I believe in good and evil and souls and auras. I told her I questioned reincarnation as such, but I do believe my current soul has been housed in another before finding me. My belief is that when you pass away, your aura of either goodness or evil is released into the universe where it takes up residence in a new life where it now becomes part of his or her soul. I explained that I wholeheartedly wished that only good auras were released, but that seems impossible as evil still exists in the world. It is not an easy thing this allowing for evil's existence as perpetuity, but if you accept the explanation of good's passing then you must accept the notion of bad's passing too, or it becomes a logical fallacy.

In addition, I believe that this other person's aura, mixed with my genetic DNA, creates a new, original person, but one who has absorbed some of his or her aura's wisdom, intuition, and instinct. For me, it explains these three innate human qualities. For instance, with regard to instinct we are born knowing how to suckle and seek out sustenance from a muscle memory needed for survival, an example of intuition may be the infamous woman's intuition for somehow knowing the correct decision at certain times and is often spoken of with reverence and respect, and as for wisdom, some of the sage decisions we make well before we have the experience from which to learn bears that out. Courtney accepted this point of view as easily as I accepted her ghosts. It was a wonderful sharing of ideas and beliefs that has stayed with me to this day because not everyone gets to have such great conversations with their niece.

I have no proof, of course, but I like to think that my soul had once been housed in an Irish girl who worked in a tavern where she had laughed and joked and served great tankards of beer. She was strong and hardworking and loyal and she was admired for those qualities. This image is clear and joyful to me, and it feels so right, I quite like the idea of accepting her prior life's aura as a part of who I am. I also feel I was a pioneer woman in some past life. I am not a girly girl whatsoever, and I have been an equal partner in all the physical work Dave and I have done in the 13 homes we have remodeled, renovated, or simply personalized. I have a tough nature and simply dig in when it is time to do so, just as a woman pioneer would have done crossing the country. As I dig in, it feels so natural and satisfying, as if it is my second nature. I wasn't raised rough and rugged, I simply am. This is all the proof I need as far as inheriting the aura/soul of several strong women. You may now be thinking about the imprudent, misguided actions I have told you about in this memoir, well, apparently along the way my prior aura's have absorbed some troublesome traits too; it seems clear this exchanging of souls is a crap shoot, so you get a blend of many past experiences, as you should. Beliefs, regardless of how you feel about the thoughts I have shared, offer an explanation, and for many of us, that is all we need.

What are your thoughts on this idea of belief systems? Am I fanciful or am I realistic? Are beliefs even to be thought of as such in the first place, you know, as real or fake? Are they meant to be true or false, right or wrong, fact or fiction…or just beliefs born from experience and personal logic held close to our hearts? As a child, I was taught that beliefs are based on simple faith; you needed no proof of God, Jesus, Mary and Joseph, immaculate conceptions, or heaven and hell. We were told this was so and that was to be enough. Our reward for this faith would be a place in heaven and the eternal happiness of God's kingdom. Though I strayed from this original belief system, I quite like that I have taken a piece of it that makes the most sense to me, and that is the idea of the possession of a soul. My interpretation of souls makes sense to me, yet I know it may be hard for others to swallow. For me it is a wonderful example of taking something from other's beliefs that you can accept, such as good and evil, and then adding your unique perspective to arrive at an explanation that fills your spiritual needs. It is easily understood why the Human Truth Foundation struggles with a finite list of accepted beliefs. There are simply too many variations of viewpoints, and they won't be listed simply because they are, like mine, personal.

Here is another belief I hold to be true. I believe in Karma. If you Google Karma, you will find quite a bit of information, but here is a succinct explanation. Karma is the law of moral causation and is a fundamental doctrine in Buddhism. Simply put, it can be explained as cause and effect. I believe what goes around, comes around—good and bad. I have plenty of proof of this as I look back at my own life, or for that matter, at very public retributions and rewards. Publically, look at the growing number of prominent men who used their power, authority, and money abusively. They are now finding themselves falling from grace, toppling hard and fast, and some think this is exactly what they deserve and brought about themselves. They are now experiencing the fear and degradation they created for someone else, men and women alike, and it is simply payback. Karma, if no good deed goes unrewarded, then it stands to reason it works the same for the bad deeds.

When I look back at the lines in the sand I crossed in life, I believe some of the bad luck I later encountered was life's way of paying me back for certain behaviors. I don't mean that in an 'eye for an eye' kind of way, but rather in a second chance kind of way. I needed to learn a lesson, and life has a way of making sure that happens. Maybe, as a lesson, I needed to experience a few setbacks such as when *I* trusted someone, and they didn't carry out their end of the bargain. After all, I had done that myself a few times when younger. Maybe, I needed to personally undergo what I had dished out myself. That is karma too and it can be a wonderful teacher. Of course, there is the good karma that comes from the times you made the morally correct choice, and you are owed the gift of good luck, or good karma. Here is a great example. The night of my graduation from Salem College, on the way out to dinner with my father, stepmother, sister and Dave, we stopped at a friend's birthday party for a drink. While at the party, I was introduced to the host's niece who congratulated me on my graduation and asked if I had a job yet. Well, the year I graduated I had been told high school English teachers were a dime a dozen; schools needed science and math teachers. I fully expected to have to apply often and meanwhile substitute teach to get my foot in a door somewhere, so I replied that No, I didn't and I was not expecting it to be an easy road She told me that there was an opening in her school, and she would call the principal and get me an interview and recommend me for the job if I wanted it. That following Monday, I had a call from the principal, I interviewed and got the job. In an extremely tough and competitive market for English teachers, I was hired three days after graduation. Now, would you say that this was simply being at the right place at the right time, or was it good Karma? I had worked hard for altruistic reasons for this career change; in addition my family had given up quite a bit themselves as so much of our life had revolved around my classes and study demands. I say it was Karma; the universe decided that my family and I deserved a break and granted me a job.

A final thought. Has your belief system changed over time? If so, maybe think about why that may be so. If not, write about why your system has been the foundation that remains a constant. Mine certainly has changed, yet I know for many the belief system embraced in their childhood, from which they never waiver, offers peace and tranquility. My good friend Anne is one such person, and witnessing her unshakeable faith has been eye opening for me. Although I was unable to find such comfort in the religion in which I had been baptized, I took teachings that made sense with me on the journey to find my own system and integrated them into my personal convictions.

I do hope you have enjoyed thinking about your belief system. I think anything that sustains us is worth talking about.

Entry #18 follows

My Thoughts and Reactions

Chapter 18
Deportment

I know, I know, you are thinking, *She's kidding, right*? But out of the clear blue this morning, while working out as a matter of fact, I felt like talking to you about how you 'carry' yourself. I was in the midst of crediting yoga with helping me with *inner* strength and I wondered if this strength showed on the *outside* too. This led me to consider how the world sees me; do they *see* my strength and how it adds to my confidence and love of life? I think it does, so I want to ask you, are you aware of how the world sees you? Step outside of yourself for a moment and see yourself from another's viewpoint. What do they observe as they watch you approach? If someone was attempting to describe your deportment to a friend, what would they say? Now, consider for a moment whether you even care how the world perceives you, or does it matter not a whit to you? Whichever side you are on, caring or not caring, your deportment itself tells the world that very choice. I've discovered that it matters to me that I am seen for whom I am, and I think it is an important subject for you to consider if you haven't done so yet. Seriously friends, have you forgiven me for using the word *deportment* yet, and will you hear me out on this vital topic? If you have stayed with me thus far, if you are still *with* me for Chapter 18, I know you will.

Webster lists deportment as a noun, so we know it's a thing. Its definition is: a behavior or way of conducting one's self. This is known as the denotation, or dictionary definition of a word, but the connotation of the word, or the emotional response the word evokes, goes way beyond the simple idea of a behavior, for it is the way you *wear* your behavior that changes everything. Over time your behavior tends to take on a persona of its own, and this is what I want us to explore a bit. For example, when I am walking down the street, on the beach, or down a hallway at school, I get reactions from people due to my deportment, and whether you realize it or not, so do you. While walking on the beach it is evident that I am extremely happy which is revealed by, as we have defined it, by the way I am carrying myself. People witness a lighthearted, free spirited woman coming toward them and their initial reaction is to smile at me, most wave at me, and many offer up a 'gorgeous day', right? Maybe I wave first at times, but whoever goes first, it is because of my body language that this little vignette of happiness plays out. As I progress down the beach, I get happier because it is all so infectious, and this *joie de vie* is spread along the coastline for the five miles of my walk. That is my perception of how others see who I am. For me, it's not just at the beach; I tend to meet people's eyes and nod and smile at everyone just about everywhere and the majority nod and smile back. I am one of those women who like to have my best foot forward at all times, and this comes across. I put on something that I feel good in, and this simple act on my part gives me a different vibe. No, I am not dolled up, but I have a sense of my comfort zone. It is definitely a big part of my deportment.

That being said, you and I know that not everyone is engaged with me in this lighthearted free-for-all and that brings me to an important point. There are others who send out a very different message with their deportment. There are those who walk with their eyes cast downward, and I can surmise by their deportment that they aren't feeling the joy I am at the moment. They may be using the beach for some healing time; this person may be internalizing something deep and they deserve to be respected, for their deportment reveals their need for privacy in this public space. It's important to note all of this simply because the rest of us need to leave them in peace in their reverie.

Do you see how this idea of deportment works and why I think it is worthy of our time? What about you? Have you begun to assess what messages you send out by how you carry yourself? I am simply asking you to think about it because your deportment is an important part of your life's interactions.

As I write, a memory rises that may prove my point. We used to camp quite a bit with a large group of friends. We were tent campers and we had it down to a science, for we had all of the basic ingredients for a fun weekend. Everyone pitched in and we cooked fantastic meals, had rafts to paddle the lakes and rivers, we went on long hikes, and we put our chairs right in the water and read our books or talked about what was on our minds. Make no mistake, it was rustic at best, but it was so relaxing. It was an outstanding time in life and the camaraderie we shared in the best of nature's bounty was a gift. I mention all of this because even on those weekends in the woods I felt the need to put my best foot forward, and for me that meant some mascara and hoop earrings. Most of my other female camper pals didn't bother, nor did they give what I did a second thought. For them it was a chance to literally let their hair down, forget the contact solution and wear their glasses and rumpled flannel shirts. But I on the other hand had my tube of mascara, I coordinated bandanas to match my flannel which I tied at the waist, I mean, why not? There were no comments from anyone in our gang on my routine because they accepted it as my deportment. It's just Eileen's way. One weekend a new couple joined us on the trip and they fit right in. However, the next morning this guy named Jim, who I liked very much by the way, looked at me with total surprise when I emerged from our tent with eye make-up, earrings, and hair arranged as best as one can in the woods. It took him a while but eventually he came and sat by me and asked me why on earth I had on eyeliner in the woods. I confess, I was taken aback for a moment, but I contemplated what the right response might be because I wanted him to understand. So, after a thoughtful pause, I answered him, "It's just me Jim; it's who I am." And do you know what? That is the simple truth of it; I have a sense of deportment, and it matters not what you think, it matters that I own it. In retrospect, I think that was a turning point for me; do what works for you and don't worry about what others may think. Carry yourself comfortably for that is what matters.

How are you feeling about this? I honestly don't assume that you agree with me on all of this, and I hope using an example with make-up as its inception doesn't weaken the impact of what I am getting at, for I do want you to consider this subject of deportment in a new light if you can. I want you to analyze how you carry yourself and most importantly why you do so in a particular manner. If we were together right now, you and I would be having a lively discussion on this subject. I am so interested in you and what makes you tick. I would seriously like to see you approaching me on the street as we meet up, so I could get a clue as to who you are by the way you carry yourself.

OK, back to it. Another anecdotal story: As a teacher, or a decorator or a salesperson for that matter, of which I was all three, there is a certain look you own that helps you feel confident and in control. I feel best in tailored, almost mannish, clothes. I like slim pants, and well cut jackets or vests. Round that out with collared shirts and I rule. I like black, and brown, and ecru, and avoid bright colors for the most part. I wore such a uniform which served well for many years as I found it professional and easy as far as mixing and matching. Let me share my personal worst look; it is a shapeless, crewneck t-shirt; I really feel out of sorts in that look and I don't buy them because I have small shoulders, heavy upper arms, and no chest to speak of. It is simply not flattering on me. When our school's administration decided we could have casual Fridays for teachers if we wore the school t-shirts, which they would provide, the cheer went throughout the halls as most folks were ecstatic. Jeans and no brainer t-shirts provided by the school! Yes please! Well, I wanted to be part of the team, and I sure wanted to wear jeans on Fridays, but those boxy, teal t-shirts (our school colors were teal and black) took some of my deportment power from me. Ever resourceful, a lifetime of sales, design, and teaching will do that for you, I found a way to make this work. Here is what I did, I wore a black golf shirt under that boxy t-shirt and then popped the collar. I rolled up the sleeves 3 times so they were capped, and then I knotted the big loose shirt to one side so now it was more fitted. Problem solved! And better yet, some teachers applauded my originality as they happily went through their day in relaxed comfort, for you see, that boxy t-shirt fit their deportment and they wore it well and owned the look.

OK, are you warming up to this subject yet? Let's shift gears and consider what happens if your deportment is off. How does your equilibrium shift and does it affect your confidence? We all accept that we have good days and bad days, but have you thought about what goes into the make-up of those days? Could we change the dynamics of a bad situation and regain control if we are consistent when it comes to how we carry ourselves?

You can almost always spot when a person is off their game or depressed or unhappy by their body language, which speaks volumes if you are attentive. As they come towards you, you can perceive how the interchange will go because this person's deportment is blaring loud and clear: hurt, angry, distressed, or depressed. You are receiving quite a bit of information as they approach; consequently, you can get your own thoughts in order as to how to proceed. This deportment is just as important as my swinging down the beach smiling my way into your life, because it sends a message, and you should pay attention to what is being relayed. In other words, don't be blinded by your personal outlook, and watch for the signals others are transmitting.

Perfect example: While in sales for VWR Scientific, all outside sales personnel were sent to a weekend workshop on personality typing. The idea was to better understand our customer base, therefore, grow sales, but I learned so much more than that on this retreat. I learned a life skill that I use to this day; the very one we are talking about. The retreat began with learning our own personality type which was fascinating in and of itself and key to understanding the course. Once we understood our personality type, we could then type our customers so we would understand their comfort zone. All of this was in the hopes we would learn to respect our customers in our approach to a better sales relationship. This simple concept did help me in sales, but it also helped me in my dealings with family, friends, and peers.

It was far more complex that this, but let's just get to the gist of it for our purposes. There are three basic personality types as taught in this particular program: A, B, and C. This may seem simplistic, but it is also effective when quickly assessing people, especially when meeting them for the first time.

Type A personalities tend to be high energy; they are continuously engaged in several thought processes at the same time and they tend to be impatient. They react quickly, and then just as quickly they may retract what they've just decided was their stance. They may seem a bit cold, yet they are passionate too. They will worry a point to death, and then just as quickly shrug it off. It is easy to have your feelings hurt by a type A if you don't understand this personality. While you are still reacting to their energy; they have already moved past whatever you are fretting over. In a business meeting you need to keep up with them, take notes and make eye contact. When your meeting or interaction is over, you feel relieved.

Type B personalities are the most common, so it encompasses a wide variety of people you meet. They are easier going by nature, and they tend to be friendly and outgoing. They make up most of the inter-personal workforce. They are typically sales people, wait staff, retail clerks, customer service, managers, and pretty much any job that needs good people skills. They tend to have patience and a willingness to make things work. They compromise to get things done. They tend not to be as egotistical as A's, but they also like success. You usually know where you stand with them and interactions are pleasant.

Type C personality types are introverted, quiet, shy, and they would rather avoid personal and social interactions. They enjoy their solitary existence. They prefer being left alone to do their own thing and avoid big, splashy events. They dress conservatively so as to not draw attention to themselves. They are usually scientists, mathematicians, researchers, analysts, and accountants. They are comfortable in a small space working intently on the job. They are highly intelligent. When dealing with them it is best to stand back, give them their space, and temper your own personality if you are an A or a B.

So that, in the proverbial nutshell as it were, is what I learned, and clearly you have figured out that I am a type B. This came as no shock to me, but a few of the Reps I was there with surprised me by coming out as C's. They shared that sales was difficult for them, but because we worked for a scientific company, they mostly called on type C's therefore were successful in their field. They crossed lines into a field that B's usually ruled in and did well because they called on their own academic personality type.

Final story: I went from Inside Sales in this company to Outside Sales. As an inside sales rep I had talked on a daily basis with the Purchasing Agents who typically were type B's like me. We had a wonderful time on our business calls, and I hadn't thought about giving credit to the fact that we were like personality types. After I was promoted and given my territory, I called on large universities, genetic research, oil refineries, and hospitals. I admit I was struggling at first, as I didn't have a strong science background, my degree was in Retail

Management, though I knew everything by name in our catalogue I didn't know how they were used in the laboratories. Here is what I discovered due to this very important workshop. My typical client was a type C and here I was blazing in all smiles and energy and laughs. I was too friendly and too outgoing and I was an intrusion. Good heavens, I wore linen suits, flowy white blouses, high heels, and you know I was wearing makeup. It was one of those smack yourself upside the head moments for me as I came to terms with the idea that I had been making them uncomfortable, and I hadn't considered this before. Being the type B I am, I determined to change my approach in order to do the right thing by them while becoming more successful for me. While sitting in waiting rooms for appointments, I now noted how the other reps calling on the account were dressed, and I found that they wore navy blue, charcoal gray or black suits. They wore pumps not heels and they wore less makeup and wore their hair simpler than my Farrah Faucette waves. Well, I am not a fool, so I heeded what my research had demonstrated was necessary and replenished my wardrobe with a more conservative look, for I now saw that my office attire as a Customer Service/Inside Sales representative wasn't appropriate for this new aspect of my career. Funny thing is that my boss had told me after my promotion that I should tone it down some, but I just thought he was being a bit stodgy. He had understood that my deportment was going to come on too strong for many of my clients, and he was right.

I have used this workshop knowledge from that time on. I use it because it is important that everyone experience comfortable encounters; don't you agree? I learned that a classic, tailored look was going to offer the best comfort zone to my clients at that time. Later, as a designer I kept it classic for clients who may have worried I was going to make their houses too bold if that is how I dressed, and finally, I dressed classically for my students who I felt needed to hear me and my lesson and not be distracted. I looked more serious and I think the kids took me as such. This worked for me as far as deportment for successful relationships in my professional life. Now as far as beach walking…well, that is a different story all together.

Has my whole tangent on deportment made more sense now that you have heard me out? If you haven't yet, please, spend some time on this idea of deportment in your journal. You may revisit an experience that didn't work out as you had hoped, and perhaps find it was because of how you carried yourself in that interaction. How could you do it differently or better next time? I am not saying that you shouldn't be yourself; of course not, but I do suggest that you think through the ways you can remain true to who you are yet temper a situation by toning down or turning on what the other person may need. Because I maintain that I am a compassionate person, this falls under that category for me. Adapting to a situation to make others feel better is not me being less than I am, just the opposite. By considering them, I am being true to who I am.

Entry #19 follows

My Responses and Reactions

Chapter 19
Bouncing Back

Yup, I am bouncing back. I know you feel it too, for you know me so well by now. And I have to admit, I can't help but wonder if you are bouncing back with me. I promise these fragment were never meant to be downers or depressing in nature but intended as valuable indulgences which we've allowed ourselves. I think we needed to do this together in order to stay balanced, sane, rational human beings, and I sure hope these fragment interactions and responses have done just that for you. Throughout this exchange of ideas and hopes and concerns and dreams, I hope you have remembered some particularly poignant moments, but I also hope you have laughed often as well. My very dear friend Linda, who reviewed the first three chapters as a favor, said she laughed and journaled with joy as she recalled how she and a friend stuffed rolled up socks in their bras just for a lark. The image of those two young Montana girls sitting atop their horses with socks bouncing in their bras as they rode is one to cherish. It is hilarious. The beauty of it is that my shameful bra-stuffing confession brought about a joyful memory for her. I found this contrasting reaction an important eye opener as I realized that this is what reading and writing and sharing could do for us. This is that other perspective I referenced way back at the beginning of our journey. I am not sure that in a casual conversation that Linda and I would have ever gotten around to talking about bra stuffing, but through reaching for your feedback to life's mysteries I ended up adding another dimension to mine and Linda's already terrific relationship. Life is just so great and random.

OK, returning to this bouncing back theory... Do you find this a positive statement, because there is no denying that in order to bounce back we have to reminisce about the fall. How many times have you had to bounce back from difficult situations or life challenging events? We've shared fragments where we have explored failure and disappointment and our recovery from such experiences, but I think we now owe it to ourselves to dedicate some time to the notion of how vital this bouncing back is to our life cycle and most importantly the resilience needed in order to achieve it. The best way to regain momentum is literally putting energy into recovery, you know what I am saying, *begin* somewhere and *do* something to rectify whatever it is that has you off kilter or out of sync.

Will you try something for me? Sit quietly and do this as you might a meditation: Imagine yourself as a ball, any size, shape, color, or type that you choose. Got it? Now throw yourself down as hard as you can and feel yourself rebounding skyward. Rise toward the light, toward the boundless horizon, soar with abandon towards some unknown height…how does it feel? At first, is it a little scary to ricochet without control? After the initial rush of fear though, will you give in to the sensation? Will you allow yourself the freedom of weightlessness and the lack of restraint? Will you allow for the sublime? This bounce back is how we regain our power and our authentic selves. We weren't put on this earth to live dormant lives, so (please forgive this very apt but iffy metaphor) do not be heavy, cumbersome medicine balls, but rather be tennis, volley, or basketballs and travel with speed and accuracy across the net and receive your well-deserved winning points.

If like me, you are finding yourself back on top, assess what brought you to this point in the first place. It could be so many different things from which we need to recover, right? Is it from a failed relationship, a job loss, or troubles with your kids or spouse? Did you begin a project into which you'd thrown your heart and soul, and before it managed to take off, the rug was pulled from under your feet? Were you forced to use your savings, which had been earmarked for a bucket list trip, and do something practical with it like a household repair? Did you lose a race you trained hard for? Did you tear your ACL and it requires surgery? There is such a variety of calamitous occurrences it boggles the mind. I want you to stop here and think about the things you have had to bounce back from. Write a few down, but don't for a moment believe I ask this of you to recount the 'bummers' of your life; no, I want you to recognize how many times you have recovered, and recovered well. I would like for you to witness your personal growth. For some of you, it may be difficult to reintroduce complicated times, but the fact that you have recovered and come out on the other side should be a boost to your morale and self-worth. It is for me.

I always do as I ask of you, so I have jotted down a few events from which I have bounced back well. Our collective list would be wide and varied and diverse wouldn't it? As the joyful socks in the bra have proven, what may have affected one person negatively is pure gold to someone else. Whatever you have written down, we are individuals with different weaknesses and strengths, so don't judge what you have listed as insignificant, because what *does* matter is that you feel you've been able to rally.

I will share one to get us rolling. I have told you that teaching was my third and favorite career. It's the truth, but it has its own story too. In the beginning of my teaching career, there was a span of time when I wondered what on earth had possessed me to have left the systematic, precise, orderly design world to enter the turbulent world of public education. You recall that I loved my education schooling, and I did very well. I got A's in my Education classes, and I felt I was as prepared as anyone could be. But because of my experience and age, I had the option to forgo doing an internship where I would have been under the wing of a highly regarded teacher, and I would have then slowly, with guidance, taken over the classroom to gain experience. It involves the quite rigorous schedule of full time work and the required classroom load of a college course. You pay college tuition for this internship, and you are not receiving a paycheck for being an intern working 8 hours a day. You can understand why at 50 years old, I opted to go right into teaching without this internship. I felt that since I had owned my own business, had many years of work under my belt, and was a parent myself, I should have the life skills for success. Let me just say now that the reality of classroom management in action is a far cry from writing your personal philosophy of it in a five-page paper for which you received an A. It was a mistake, my friends, to forego an internship, but one I didn't know at that time.

There were one or two stumbling blocks from the get-go, for the high school where I would begin teaching was a 45-minute ride away from my home, and I had to be there by 7:10 a.m. I left way before my sons were up, so it would fall to their father to get them up and off to school. I was worried about it, but I knew many families who had to share this responsibility and we would adjust like everyone else. I did my best to have everything ready the evening before, so at least it could run as smoothly as possible. Jake was in 7th grade so pretty self-sufficient, and Josh was in 5th, so it's not like they were babies, but I still felt a pang of guilt because I had always put them first, and now I was putting other kids, my students, first. Remember however, this was my good karma job, and so off I drove believing in my heart all was meant to be.

Here is how it went: I taught all freshmen classes, and they are a squirrely lot by nature. They hit my classroom like a tornado with all the excitement of their first day: seeing friends, being cool, and nervously loud. My classes were large, and it was difficult to get their attention, but finally I do manage that. I want to get right to teaching, but there is so much housekeeping that must be done for a school opening that what I really knew how to do well had to be put aside while attendance, seating charts, passing out books, and locker assignments consume us. It is already apparent whose seats need to be moved as I have them in alphabetical order and clearly many know each other well and begin to act foolishly. Classroom Management 101 tells me to be firm and stern as you can always get nicer but not tougher as far as gaining control of kids. They will spot weakness a mile away, so I have to bark a bit and I do. I had really wanted to earn their respect, and when I did this, I just knew that they would do what was right because they liked me. See a fatal flaw here? Foolish woman, I was thinking like an optimistic adult and I was dealing with squirrelly fourteen-year-olds on the first day of school. The bell rings and that class rushes off and before I can catch my breath or use the bathroom, in march 30+ more squirrely kids. We rinse and repeat and my head is spinning, and I feel I have gotten nowhere. I am simply holding on…another bell… another group…another bell, another group. Wait, can it please be lunch so I can go use the bathroom? Lesson number 1; don't drink a big mug of coffee on your 45-minute ride to work. Lunch whizzes by and another group comes in. Finally, my last class leaves, and I realize I know no one's name, their faces are a blur, I have a mountain of paperwork to organize, and I didn't get attendance down to the main office as required, so I am already in a bit of hot water. I check my mailbox which is full of important documents for the kids with special needs, illnesses, IEP's, and 504's, and because I am a new teacher, I have to stay after school for the first 3 weeks with my mentor and qualify for my ILT point quota. I need to master the school's computer system for entering grades and eventually attendance, I have been assigned to guard the girls bathroom before and after 1st period for the first week, there are many faculty meetings as it is a new year with many changes ahead, I discover I am an EOC teacher, so my kids have to pass a standardized test with a certain score or not move on to their sophomore year for English. I need to do the dreaded daily 6point lesson plan and hand it in to the principal at the end of the week, and I have been assigned to take money at the gate after school for some sport I don't even remember. This was day number one my friends, and I drove that long road home close to tears and in shock. You see, everyone else was doing all I was doing, and they were just as busy, the only difference was that it was normal for them. They didn't check in on me throughout the day because I was a bona fide teacher, and they must have assumed that I knew all about school openings. I did not. I had opted out of the internship program, and I was truly lost without that dress rehearsal. By the time I got home, though, I was in a better frame of mind and got myself organized for the next day, where surely I would teach English, and the kids would see a really accomplished person standing before them.

Here is how the rest of the week went: One of the kids cussed me out and put his big work boots on the desk and tipped back in in his chair in defiance. Another young man said intentionally loud that I had pretty decent boobs for an older lady (note to self, no fitted sweaters), some girls started to eat lunch in my classroom so they could save their lunch money for ammo to go squirrel hunting on the weekends, I discovered the plastic bottles in the kids flannels shirts were not bottles of ice tea, but spit bottles and kids were chewing in the back of the room. I discover that though I know my grammar, I now have to put it in such a way that the kids will understand it too, and I learned not everyone liked the short stories I found so compelling. I really feel like I am failing, and it is noticeable in my body language and I do ask for help, and everyone is kind but they are as busy as me, and I am not the only new teacher in the English Department. Apparently, in their eyes I was doing extremely well compared to a young man they had hired who was already calling in sick because he had ended up with the toughest kids and was shell-shocked. For the entire first month I drove to school determined to do better, and then the entire way home sick at heart, frustrated, and miserable, for this was not what I had signed on for; this was nothing like I had imagined. This was almost as bad as boot camp! But then my friends it happened, just as it had in boot camp, I found my stride. The day arrived when the 6-point lesson plan hit home; I saw light bulbs going off in my kid's heads as far as comma rules were concerned, they said they liked the short story *The Sniper*, I had finally mastered the computer system and made friends with the copier woman. I took my kids outside to the bleachers where we wrote Found Poems, and I had learned to love my lunch bunch girls as they were as sweet as could be, the teacher next door took to coming by on his planning period to give me tips, and I learned to use the commute as an opportunity to *review* the day and *reflect* on ways I could tweak and improve a lesson. The kids began to demonstrate that they liked me, I started to joke more and lightened up, I gave out compliments every day for the most minor of things just to make someone feel good. I had rid the class of spit bottles; they had taken my largest class of 35 and got it down to 25...I was bouncing back! I walked the hallways smiling at everyone and found that the dreaded 6-point plans were helping me stay organized and focused on goals and objectives. I learned to manage my time well, and I now did all of the things expected of a teacher with confidence and enthusiasm; we renewed our social life, I found that Jake and Josh were fine, and though Dave didn't get them out the door as I had, they got out the door and were probably gaining some needed independence. You see, nothing about the circumstances changed, it was my attitude that changed everything. I was now the damn ball and I was soaring toward the horizon and loving it. The point is that you can't overstay the down times, so wallow for a spell in your misery if you must, but then get your act together and snap out of it. Are you feeling this? I know you are. I finished up that rookie year on a high, and was asked back, but I decided to try to work closer to home. I got hired at a new school in my county and entered the finest English Department one could have asked for. My good karma continued, and my teaching career became all I had dreamt it would be. I made this happen by **bouncing back**.

I will tell you another bounce back episode, but I will also tell you now that this one took longer than a month or two for me to get my mojo back. This time my ego was involved and apparently it takes much longer when you unexpectedly fail at something in a public way, particularly when you had never allowed for anything but success. Here is my story.

After happily teaching for seven years, I decided it was time to improve my credentials. My choices were to get my Master's Degree in Teaching or to become a National Board Certified teacher. A Masters required returning to school, but Certification had a different approach as it required a rigorous process of analysis of your practices as a teacher and then writing critical thinking essays critiquing them. You were required to film two different lessons showing mastery of your goals and objectives as laid out for the board. When completed, you submitted these entries for grading. There were also computer generated prompts which required on the spot lessons plans for a proposed teaching challenge. You were expected to attain a certain cumulative score between the two formats in order to be recognized as a Board Certified teacher. Both a Masters and Certification offered a pay increase upon completion, which is always a nice incentive, and truthfully, I decided on National Boards over a Masters because I believed I could do it faster, and there were state scholarships available for those who went this route. North Carolina was promoting Board Certified teachers as an asset to the state's commitment for high standards at this time and schools encouraged this route. It seemed like the better choice for me as I could do it on my own time and not have to attend evening or on-line classes for my Masters. I had heard that Board Certification was a bear, but I also felt I wasn't that long out of school and my good study habits and commitment to excellence would carry me through. I did seek advice from those who had already been through the process, and I found a local mentor who was willing to offer her time on weekends to go over my entries, so undauntedly I signed up and went to work. It turned out there was indeed a timeframe involved because there are only so many testing dates for Boards, but I do like a little pressure and really wasn't overly concerned about handling it. There were eight of us attempting Boards at my school, and we commiserated and cried a bit on each other's shoulders over the workload, but we also cheered each other on. I do want to share that it was proving very challenging for me, yet it never once crossed my mind that I wouldn't pass. Ole Pollyanna Eileen even began to think she would get such high scores that she would surpass her own expectations…maybe I would become a mentor for future teachers attempting their Boards? Oh, such lofty thoughts danced in my head. I had been such a good student at Salem College that I incorrectly assumed that this would be relatively easy for me. It was not. It was long and arduous and frustrating. You had to color inside the lines and check all of the boxes, which you now know is not my forte. Sometimes it went against my altruistic reasons for becoming a teacher because I felt I was encouraged to write what they wanted, not what *I* believed in. I spent every spare moment on it for it had become all consuming, and it was not at all enjoyable like the professor led classes had been for me in college. It was too late to change my mind though, and so I soldiered on, again, never thinking for a moment that the committee wouldn't see my passion for my kids and my subject and pass me with high scores. I submitted my work, and took the computer test aspect of it, and relaxed and waited for those passing scores to be returned.

Oh my friends, you have long since known where this story was going haven't you? Well, you are right, I did not pass. But what you don't know is that I not only didn't pass, I had such low scores on three of my entries that I had to redo them completely. Ironically, it was the three entries in which I felt that I done my best work. Man, I haven't talked about this in a long time, maybe I never admitted how shocking this failure was until telling you, what a kick in the gut it was or how humiliated I felt. I was offered the opportunity to redo the three entries and the support of a mentor to work with. I would have to pay for them as the state wouldn't pay out twice, and this amounted to several thousand dollars. I was so unprepared for any of this and my heart just sagged at the idea of beginning again. Of the eight of us, four had passed and four of us had not. I am ashamed to admit I found some comfort in the fact that others hadn't passed as well, for you know misery loves company. My principal had even sent me a congratulatory email on my Certification before he realized I was one of the ones who hadn't pass. It was so expected I would make it; I think many were as shocked as I was.

Well, in a large, busy school, the next distraction is a basketball game, or suspension, or Academic Team win away, and those of us who hadn't passed quickly fell from the headlines, but I couldn't shake the shock and disappointment. For a while, it didn't seem to matter that I was respected by my peers, that my kids passed state tests with good scores, that my lesson plans went over well, or that I taught with passion and compassion. The question remained, "What the heck had gone so wrong Eileen?" Well friends, if you want to bounce back and regain your mojo, you need to find the answer to that question. Weirdly though, this search is not like tearing the scab off of the wound, it's actually very healing. It's more like stitches, it stings a bit, but then it helps the all-important closure of the wound. So I had a 'come to Jesus' meeting with myself about what had taken place. What I had to acknowledge was that I hadn't really listened to my mentor well enough. When she had critiqued my lesson videos and made suggestion for changes, I didn't make them. In fact, I rebelled against them because I felt what I had produced was exactly what the Board wanted. I should have accepted her sage advice because she was the authority on this. She knew what evidence of good practices the committee was looking to identify in the video and her advice had had merit; it had been sound. Think about this, how many of your bounce back sagas may be self-inflicted? You know what I am getting at, the ones of your own making. My recovery began the moment I accepted that I had not listened to wiser counsel, that I had let the old pigheaded Eileen take over. My god, is that pigheaded girl to stay with me forever? But there it was, that was the ball, and so once again I threw it down and decided to get over myself and be what I already knew to be true, certified or not, I was a damn fine teacher. Did I ever finish the process? Well, I could only afford to do one test at a time without scholarships, and I did rewrite and resubmit one. I passed, but not with glowing scores, so when it came time to face the next two, I found myself reluctant and certainly not enthusiastic, and I decided I would take off a semester. And then, just when I needed it most, the universe delivered me an opportunity of mentoring a student teacher's internship from, of all schools, my alma mater Salem College. I threw all of my love of teaching, my acquired skills, my years of experience, and my passion for English at this young man; we went on to have the best possible semester together, for it's true what Mick Jagger sings, *"You can't always get what you want, no, you can't always get what you want, but if your try sometimes, you just might find, you get what you need."* A huge part of my bouncing back was getting what I needed, and how I needed you Tom Peterson. I let finishing Boards slip away, and I found peace within again. In bouncing back, sometimes we find we have to let go of that bone clenched in our teeth. Bouncing back may not always appear in the guise of soaring toward the horizon; it may be as simple as rediscovering who you are and rejoicing in that.

I hope you have looked hard at times when you have bounced back from disappointment or despair. We all have hard times, many more than two, and we all need to rise from the ashes of them and regain our zest for life. If you haven't yet, do try to express yourself on the following pages. It may just be that you are in need of a bounce back right now, or you may currently be in a position to encourage someone by sharing your bouncing back-story with them.

Entry #20 follows

My Responses and Reactions

Chapter 20
A Fond Farewell

Oh my dear, beloved friends, I feel our time together, for this series of fragments at any rate, is coming to its conclusion. I feel that I have asked so much of you thus far, and I worry that if I keep at you, it will diminish what we have accomplished together. This once seemingly improbable adventure of mine, one I began writing by the seat of my pants years ago, has had a profound impact on me. I am not the same person I was before sharing these odds and ends, these fragments, with *you*. I began with such trepidation...who was I to believe my life stories mattered? But then, I may as well ask who are you to write yours? Well, we are the everywoman, that's who we are, and we matter most because we are the heart and soul of society. We are the cultural norm and we keep the world spinning on its axis. You and I know this. We know our value though the world may not know **us**. So I ask my last series of questions with hope, has this been a worthy voyage for you too? Has responding to these fragments helped you resolve old issues? Have you shared a few laughs at yourself from the perspective of a more mature, wiser you? Andrea, a wonderful kindred spirit who has read this cover to cover, admitted choking up a few times as she responded to a particular prompt; I confess I have too, especially when I was editing Heroes and Heroines. While editing, there were times I was tempted to rewrite parts of a fragment to soften the blow; some of it felt so raw, yet it was never the point of this conversation to sugarcoat reality, and I hope that you did not either. I have also reaffirmed many of my life's convictions while talking with you and yet I still find myself struggling with a few unresolved issues. I know I will continue to seek your advice as I work on them. I sense what you have written me is diverse, fascinating, and important, and I value you and your time. In teaching, we say that if we help even one child, we have done our job. Well, if even one fragment has helped you, then I will feel like I have done mine.

I began this to reach out to you, whoever and wherever you are. I soon found I wasn't content simply knowing you were out there; I wanted to find you and I wanted an interaction with you. I suspect this is how all writing begins, this craving for interaction. Do writers share the same need to communicate in hopes of reaching some soul that will answer, "Yes, yes I understand you, and thank heavens you understand me." I have been lucky enough (or is it karma?) throughout my life to find kindred spirits through literature, art, music, and nature, and we have written about these very topics together. As I write this now, beautiful music is on in the background fortifying and reinforcing me. I have never met the artist playing, but the music clearly speaks to me; soothing me, it spurs me on. It encourages me as I continue my effort to create something of value, something noteworthy. I consider the effort they've expended to *finish* the score, and furthermore, to *find* someone who believes in them to produce it. Looking around the house I note that my walls are adorned with beautiful, unique pieces that spoke to me/us amongst the many in the gallery, or art show, or craft fair. What prompted these artists to continue to pursue their creative side? Did they know I was out here, and that once I saw it, I would want to possess it for my own? I don't think it is random luck because my home has come together, as if by a master design, to create this serene setting in which we live. I think of it as a collaboration born of my kindred spirits' works. While creating art, music, or verse, are we doing it for ourselves, or are we doing it for you? For me, I have discovered it is for both of us. It is an absorbing pursuit, this creative side of one's self; it requires constant feeding and nurturing. It demands attention; it tugs at your shirttails, it wakes you up at night; and it also calms and pacifies you. It changes you.

Yes, if you are reading this, some publisher read my thoughts and decided you may want to also. Someone believed that this was worth your time. I believe this is worth your time, but how to get this to you so you can decide what is worthy or not. Will you believe me if I say it is not for fame or glory that I write you? I think you will, because you have come to know me very well by now. My reasons remain altruistic, for I find I want *you* to shake off your heavy loads, and I want *you* to understand that I *get you*. I honestly labor to connect with you, to talk with you. But now comes the hard part; I need to take action and do something with this manuscript. Actually, a while ago, I decided I needed to get advice from sources I trusted, and I began searching for the right course of action that would calm my lingering doubts. Here is what I did, and I wonder if you would have done the same in my situation.

Because I felt a certain amount of unease when it came to the clarity of my *voice,* I asked a diverse group of friends to interact with the first three chapters. They were to read them through and respond to my questions and journal prompts. I know I know...*friends* you are thinking won't tell you the truth; they will spare your feelings rather than hurt you. I worried a bit too, but decided it was worth a chance. If you remember the chapter on friendships, you will understand that I did not ask acquaintances, but lifetime friends who would give me honest feedback, and their reactions were as varied and diverse and honest as they themselves are. The thing that I cared most about was whether or not they each heard the 'voice' behind the fragment, and I think that is all any writer, or want-to-be writer, hopes for. If your reader can't *hear* you, then you have failed them. The idea behind this memoir has always been to reach you, so if these initial readers did not find themselves engaged or drawn in, then I would have fallen short of my goals for us all. Happily, I was encouraged by their individual responses and by the fact that each of them felt they had heard the voice. As I had hoped, their reactions were varied because of their unique personalities. I took it as a sign that I had not only succeeded in piquing their curiosity but had led them down some paths of personal exploration that they found gratifying as well as disconcerting. My friend's receptivity sanctioned my belief that I was onto something and I should continue, which clearly I have.

Right now I am seeking some words of wisdom and encouragement that will help me, you, us, through what must next be done. I think I have the resolve to get this out to one, two, three, maybe a hundred publishers. I think I will even try the one hundred and first because what if they are the ones who hear what no one else has before? Remember, I am not a quitter and it occurs to me that this will either work well for me, or break my heart because we will never meet. Regardless, I have to do it simply because I do.

Right now I know I am over editing this manuscript as I try to say goodbye to you. I know this because there are only so many ways to rework a sentence or select the best word choice for clarity. I can't seem to stop myself though, and I promise myself I will stop on certain dates and then I don't. I suppose each day I don't say goodbye to you will just prolong what I told you from the beginning felt inevitable. If you were here with me right now, I know you would tell me to just go for it and fulfill my dream. Of course you would, so I am going to listen to you my lifetime friends.

I know I need to tear the Band-Aid of you off quickly now that I have admitted that. When I was younger I used to get into the cold pool one step at time rather than plunge in, and that was just foolishness, but like entering that cold pool I am finding this quite difficult. It seems so decisive, this final plunge, yet I don't want to blather on at you, for you will know the difference.

I so wanted to end with something dramatic and dynamic, and I think I have come upon the right ending for us, though the words be not mine the story is.

Final story: As a teacher, you feel this rather intense desire to leave some profound ideal with your kids. Something they can unpack weeks, months, or years later in the hopes it will prove to be a needed lifeline. While teaching my seniors, this seemed particularly important to me, especially when battling the infamous *Senioritus*. There was a poem that I dearly loved by the Pulitzer Prize winner Gwendolyn Brooks which I believed would be the best farewell message I could offer these students who I had come to love, but I also knew it may be lost amongst all of the excitement and stress of graduation if I tried to *teach* it and its significance. What I decided to do was to type the poem out, and with the help of my beloved friend and Media Center specialist Sarah, we printed and laminated the poem and turned it into bookmarks. Then I sat down with my rosters, and I wrote each student a personal note recounting some interaction that we had experienced that year. I thanked them for the role they'd played in my life. I inserted this note and bookmark into envelopes and handed them out the last few days of school. The truth is I do not know if or when they fully understood this poem's importance for I hadn't translated or explained each line as I would have in a lesson plan. But, I hope for some, maybe even just one, the day came that they fully comprehended what Brooks was saying. Today, as it happens, is my full awakening.

Speech to the Young, Speech to the Progress-toward

Say to them,
Say to the down-keepers
The sun-slappers
The self-spoilers
The harmony hushers
"even if you are not ready for day
it cannot always be night"
You will be right
For that is the hard homerun
Live not for battles won
Live not for the end-of-story
Live in the along.

My night is apparently over, and it appears I am ready for the day. Publishers, here I come.

Epilogue follows.

Epilogue
Denouement

Sometimes at the end of a novel or short story, the author may offer his or her reader a denouement, which is the outcome of a series of events. May I offer you this as a form of closure, although I think we can agree that in life there is no real closure for us, only an ending of these twenty chapters of our life's fragments, for I feel we will meet again some sunny day?

As of this writing, I still:

Value my favorite traits as those of passion and compassion.

All of my brothers and sisters still walk this earth, but my beloved, larger-than-life, 97-year-old father passed away while this was at the publishers being proofed. He was so proud of what I have accomplished, and he couldn't wait to get the first copy hot off the press. I will give it to my lovely stepmother, Margot, who loved him and cared for him until he passed away in their home.

I found as the years rolled on that I rather enjoyed my smaller breasts and the freedom they offered from things like deep strap grooves in my shoulders, the ease with which I could buy tops, and fewer back troubles.

I watch young people struggle with their loss of innocence with kindness and patience as it is apparently a required curse.

I continue to value and share my defining moments as a measure of the trust I feel toward people.

I have NOT found myself. I am not content!

My friends remain the pillars upon which my foundation dwells.

My many loves flourish and grow exponentially; my favorite love is still saved for my sons, Jake and Josh, who are growing and changing and working at being wonderful young men.

I find success in my newfound ability to drift aimlessly at times.

I choose truth at all times, but I have learned to temper my delivery as a measure of respect.

My list of heroes and heroines continues to grow, and I hope that the list grows as long as I live for that means the qualities of heroes and heroines lives on.

I continue to fiercely believe that Choice is everyone's given right. Even though at times I disagree with your choices, I honor your right to them. I expect that you will honor mine.

Oh yes, I have proclaimed **never** a few additional times as I told you I would, but I quickly take it back!!! I find a way to reframe that blasphemous word.

I have discovered there is no limit as to how far I will go. I would like to believe that my mental fortitude knows no boundaries in this area, as long as it remains safe and sane. BTW Dave loved his workshop and found some comfort and solace there.

We are struggling with saving our marriage. Dave and I have not been able to maintain our commitment which is difficult to admit.

My belief system still offers me the spiritual and academic relief I seek. It gives me options and I bend and sway as I continue to seek new, fresh ideas in this area.

And oh, my friends, my deportment is better than ever! I am coming into my own in ways I could never have known but trusted I would because I heeded my friend Jackie's words that the best is yet to come.

I am the ball and I am still soaring somewhere, I know not yet, but somewhere wonderful awaits my entrance into its atmosphere.

Finally, I can never thank you enough for softening me, for rounding me out, for hearing my *voice.*

Happy Trails to you, keep smiling on till then…

Happy Trails to you until we meet again (Dale and Roy)

Entry #21 follows, last but least…

My Responses and Reactions and Denouement

_____

_____

_____

_____

_____

_____

_____

_____

_____

_____

_____

_____

_____

_____

_____

_____

_____

_____

_____

_____

_____

_____

_____

Off the cuff songs which I love in no particular order:

Brown Eyed Girl-Van-Morrison, *Moon Dance* Van-Morrison, *I Did It My Way*-Frank Sinatra, *Mack the Knife*-Bobby Darin, *Bridge Over Troubled Water*-Simon and Garfunkel, *Free Bird*-Lynyrd Skynyrd, *Another Brick in the Wall*-Pink Floyd, *American pie*-Don McLean, *Born to Run*-Bruce Springsteen, *Jungle Land*-Bruce Springsteen, *I Feel Like a Woman*-Shania Twain, *All my Loving*-The Beatles, *Piano Man*-Billy Joel, *Californian Dreaming*-Mama and the Papas, *Desperado*-The Eagles, *Sympathy for the Devil*-Rolling Stones, *This Ole* Cowboy-Marshall Tucker, *Good Riddance* (The Time of Your Life)-Green Day, *Boulevard of Broken Dreams*-Green Day, *Beautiful Day*-U2, *Brothers in Arms*-Dire Straits, *Born to be Wild*-Steppenwolf, *People*-Barbara Streisand, *Evergreen*-Barbara Streisand Every song in the Sound of Music...

-Books I love that have greatly impacted me in no certain order:

Atlas Shrugged and *Fountain Head* by Ayn Rand

Dear and Glorious Physician and *Captains and Kings* by Taylor Caldwell

Lords of Discipline and *The Prince of Tides* by Pat Conroy

The Book Thief by Markus Zusak

To Kill a Mockingbird by Harper Lee

Pride and Prejudice by Jane Austen

Frankenstein by Mary Shelly

The Color Purple by Alice Walker

Rebecca by Daphne du Maurier

Dr. Zhivago by B Pasternak

The Road by Cormac McCarthy

The Rent Collector by Camron Wright

A Gentleman in Moscow by Amor Towles

The Kite Runner by Khaled Hosseini

The Language of Flowers by Vanessa Diffenbaugh

Still Alice by Lisa Genova

A Separate Peace by John Knowles

Gone with the Wind by Margaret Mitchell

CPSIA information can be obtained
at www.ICGtesting.com
Printed in the USA
BVHW040726071119
563135BV00007B/51/P

9 781528 936378